ADVENTURE MAPS TO
BUILD AND EXPLORE IN
MINECRAFT®

ADVENTURE MAPS TO
BUILD AND EXPLORE IN
MINECRAFT®

KIRSTEN KEARNEY

MITCHELL
BEAZLEY

Adventure Maps to Build and Explore in Minecraft®
by Kirsten Kearney

An Hachette UK Company
www.hachette.co.uk

First published in Great Britain in 2017 by Mitchell Beazley,
a division of Octopus Publishing Group Limited,
Carmelite House
50 Victoria Embankment
London EC4Y 0DZ
www.octopusbooks.co.uk

Front cover images, clockwise from top left: The Tourist, Loic Serra;
Rollerquester, Hans Verdolaga/Michael Anderson; The Asylum,
Sunfury; Spaghetti Rollercoaster, Daniel Pe/Michael Anderson

Back cover images, clockwise from top left: Infinity Dungeon,
Tim Gehrig; Eronev 2: Soul Cauldron, Tim Gehrig; The Jugglers
Balls, Tim Gehrig; La Brocanterie, Schnogot.

A CIP record for this book is available
from the British Library.
ISBN 978-1-78472-272-2

This book was conceived, designed, and produced by
Quintet Publishing Limited
4th Floor Ovest House
58 West Street
Brighton, East Sussex
BN1 2RA
United Kingdom

Designer: Allen Boe
Art Director: Michael Charles
Project Editor: Chris Gatcum
Senior Editor: Caroline Elliker
Editorial Director: Emma Bastow
Publisher: Mark Searle

Printed and bound in China
10 9 8 7 6 5 4 3 2 1

Printed in China by Toppan Leefung

CONTENTS

WELCOME TO ADVENTURE MAPS

When I started work on this book I was looking forward to learning more about Minecraft® and its community. But as I spoke to more and more people about creating adventures within the framework of the game, I realised that it's not really a book about Minecraft at all. It's a book about people telling stories, and the thrill they get from firing the imagination of others: what Minecraft provides is the perfect platform for this.

But Minecraft doesn't just provide a stage for creating adventures for other people to play. It's more nuanced than that. In the books, *Create and Construct: Incredible Minecraft Cities* and *Create and Construct: Super Structures in Minecraft*, I look at how Minecraft can be employed as a 3D modelling tool that requires no training to use. The structures and cities we can make in the game access the architect in our mind, allowing us to bypass many of the complex traditional tools needed to visualise and make solid our castles in the air. The game is a gateway.

In *Adventure Maps* you will see that this holds true for game development as well. Programming, coding, level design and mechanics are often so unwieldy in the world of game design that it requires several years of training even to begin to understand it all. In Minecraft you still use programming, but it is given form; each action is a block. If you want to know what two plus two is you have the blocks in front of you and you count them up.

This is the nuanced part: it's not about making game design easy, it's about making it *accessible*. Think of all those people with fantastic ideas in their heads for wonderful games to play, but who don't have the tools or experience to make them a reality. They might be too young or have too many other responsibilities in life to be able to dedicate the years to game design study. Yet with Minecraft, all of these people have a way to create adventures for us. Privilege and fortune no longer dictate who can make video games. That's a big deal. Think what we would have missed out on if people in disadvantaged circumstances hadn't been able to access paint and canvas or musical instruments.

Yet as accessible as making adventures in Minecraft is, there is still a huge amount of energy, organisation and passion needed to actually make a game that will delight the player. That is what really shines through in these pages, with fantastic games from some incredibly vivacious individuals. Even when they think they have done as much as they possibly can to make their work shine, their creativity begins to bubble again. One of the most brilliant and spirited adventure makers I've met on this journey, 'Jigarbov', told me that his latest game, *City of Love 2,* would be his last. He says his stories are exhausted and he's pushed Minecraft as far as it can go. He says that after every game.

– Kirsten Kearney

THE STORY OF MINECRAFT®

Minecraft is aptly named, as it's all about mining and crafting: you break and place blocks to create new things. The blocks are cubes that represent dirt, stone, wood, ores and water, which can be mined from the procedurally generated world you arrive in when you begin your game. This basic concept was released publicly as an unfinished game by Swedish programmer Markus 'Notch' Persson on May 17, 2009.

At first, this creative mode of play had no fixed purpose or guidance. Players simply broke blocks and placed them to create new structures, offering a sandbox gaming experience that encouraged emergent play – it was up to the players to decide what to do for themselves.

The one thing that is more fun than messing around in a game aimlessly is messing around in a game with your friends, so a multiplayer mode quickly followed. Notch then implemented a 'Survival mode', which gave the game a sense of danger and urgency. Building became a matter of necessity, as players needed to protect themselves from the dangers of zombies and skeletons in the night! Even at this early stage, more and more people were starting to notice the potential of this simple little game.

After a few mentions in the games press in September 2010, Minecraft's web server crashed under the weight of new players signing up. Notch made the game free to download at this point, to compensate players for the crash, but this only served to increase the number of new players signing up daily.

Then came the 'mega builders'. A 1:1 perfect replica of the Starship Enterprise created in Minecraft went viral, and as Twitter lit up with talk about the game and YouTube started to fill with new and ever more imaginative builds, its popularity increased exponentially. Regular updates meant that players felt they were a part of the development process of the game, leading them to suggest new and exciting ways to create structures.

With 16 million users registered before the game was even officially released, when it finally launched in November 2011 it was an instant hit, garnering a slew of awards. The game was a critical and commercial hit and went on to sell 54 million copies.

Today, Minecraft boasts its own annual global convention, MineCon, which has been running since 2010. The game has also been used as an educational and tech application in various schools and universities around the world; it is even being used to create a full replica of the British Museum, including all of its exhibits!

From Minecraft's simple blocks, elaborate worlds can be created: for *Symbiosis* (pages 90–95) Everbloom Studios created a large and detailed organic environment.

TOOLS AND BLOCKS

There are hundreds of different types of blocks available in Minecraft®; some can be mined, such as ores and plants, while others are manufactured by crafting them. Items such as tools can also be crafted to speed up the mining process. All tools have a durability and will take damage the more they arc used. Wood, stone, iron and diamond tools have increasingly better durability.

However, in Creative mode all blocks and items are available in your inventory in infinite quantities. These are used by builders in all kinds of interesting ways to create structures and re-create recognisable 'real' items.

Below is a selection of the tools and materials that are available to you.

TOOLS

Compass	Diamond sword	Flint & steel	Gold axe	Iron spade	Item frame
Sign	Stone pickaxe	Water bucket	Wooden hoe	Lava bucket	Music disc

MATERIALS

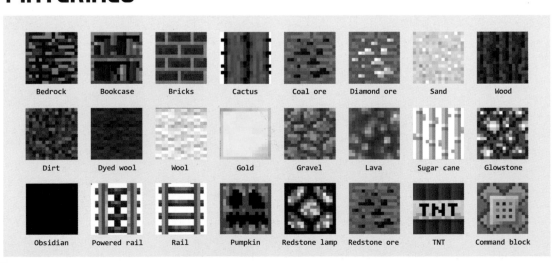

Bedrock	Bookcase	Bricks	Cactus	Coal ore	Diamond ore	Sand	Wood
Dirt	Dyed wool	Wool	Gold	Gravel	Lava	Sugar cane	Glowstone
Obsidian	Powered rail	Rail	Pumpkin	Redstone lamp	Redstone ore	TNT	Command block

For this prison-themed project, simple clean stone slabs deliver an aggressive look that is designed to induce depression in the inmates!

Layered stained glass can build an object that seems like it's not really there!

Wood is one of the main materials used in this Japanese-themed world.

Limiting your build to a few coloured blocks can create a striking effect.

THE PHYSICS OF MINECRAFT®

Minecraft may be a simple block-building game, but its physics (or lack of them) provide a clever set of rules and logic of their own, which makes building fun and intuitive. Simply put, if you build three blocks high and then knock out the lowest block, the ones above will not fall. Instead, they will stay in their position. You can pass under floating blocks and stand on top of them. They won't be affected by weight.

This simple rule, which applies to most of the blocks in-game, provides a way of building that is fast and enables processes that anyone can easily master. A good example is creating a solid wall and then punching out blocks to create entranceways and windows. Building in the real world, whether with bricks and mortar or toy building blocks, doesn't work like this, but in the digital world it makes perfect sense.

There is a number of exceptions, though. As beautiful as a perfectly sculpted object is, almost all builders like to add dynamic entities to their structures. Therefore, the few blocks that do have rules attached to them create opportunities to add movement and interaction with what would otherwise be a lifeless model.

One of the most common elements to add 'life' is fire. Torches offer a simple light source, while lava (and water) can be directed to flow in a particular way to lend a sense of nature to builds. Conversely, gravel and sand offer the more traditional physical element of having weight. They will not float when dug out from underneath as other blocks do.

Stairs are one of the most common building blocks. They can be merged at right angles to create transitions in builds that can't quite be achieved with normal blocks.

There are also blocks with more complex properties that can be used in a range of imaginative ways. This type of block includes TNT and pressure pads, but perhaps the most interesting is redstone, as outlined on page 22.

However, while new objects, tools and mods have become available over the years, changing Minecraft a little bit each time, the fundamental physics remain the same. As you will see in this book, with just a few simple rules almost anything can be created!

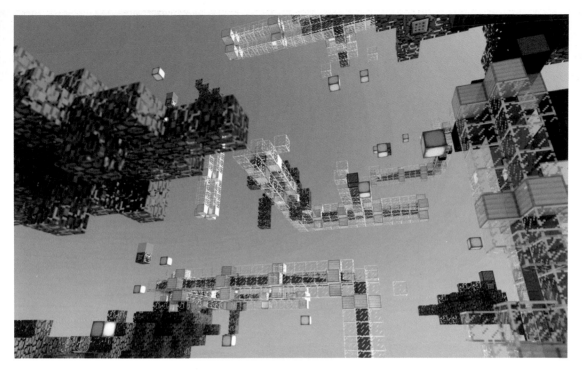

Although a lot of Minecraft builds aim for a certain level of realism, the game isn't limited by the physics of the real world. *Just Escape* (above; pages 240-247) and *Cube Block* (below; pages 152-157) both provide players with a gravity defying playing environment.

ADVENTURE MAPS AND EMERGENT PLAY

Minecraft® was not the first game to introduce the idea of a 'digital sandbox', in which you can create your own little sandcastles and make your own imaginary worlds. However, as technology has progressed, this type of game has become more and more popular. With it, game developers have helped us to fulfil our desire to create our own scenarios.

Long before this type of open world game was possible, gamers were finding ways to use the simplest of mechanics, glitches and destructive play to 'bend' games to their will. They would complete levels without using the jump button or find ways through invisible walls to finish games without collecting important items. It was a thrill to have usurped the intentions of the designer in any way possible, and in this small way people were making their own games.

Yet while Minecraft encourages you to do your own thing, it was designed with a basic goal in mind: the player would collect materials and build some kind of shelter. Although that idea evolved in a plethora of visually stunning ways, it was not long before players did what they always do, and began to make their own goals.

It started with mazes and invented games such as *Spleef*, where destroying blocks below other players would cause them to fall off the playing field (with the last player on the field declared the winner). Although many of these games were rudimentary, they proved that the player was ultimately in control of the game, and the master of their environment. In celebration, more and more elaborate mazes were designed and increasingly outrageous *Spleef* arenas appeared.

Today, redstone and command blocks have handed over the keys to Minecraft to the players in a way never before seen in a video game. The technical ability to create adventures for ourselves has allowed us to make an infinite variety of scenarios, tell each other stories, and challenge one another in increasingly imaginative ways.

WHAT IS EMERGENT PLAY?

Like many games, Minecraft relies on quite simple game mechanics. However, this has not stopped players from creating complex scenarios, narratives and behaviours that were not necessarily thought out in advance by the game's designer. This process is now known as 'emergent play.'

PLATFORM CHOICE

Although there's only one Minecraft game, it is available for several platforms: PC, consoles and portable (there's also a specialist 'Minecraft Pi' version for the Raspberry Pi, but that's pretty niche).

With all the different platforms come different operating systems and device-specific options, which means you can play Minecraft on a wide range of tech. With the portable edition of the game, for example, you can play on the go using an Android, iOS, or Windows Phone device. The console editions have versions for XboxOne, XBox 360, PS4, PS3, WiiU and the handheld Playstation Vita.

However, while this lets you play the game on your device of choice, none of these platforms allow the same level of modding or cross-platform compatibility as the PC version. This was the first version of Minecraft to be released, and the most versatile when it comes to building, modding and playing adventure games. So, while you can play Minecraft on a huge range of devices, if you want to emulate the builds in this book or play them, you need to be running the PC version of Minecraft on a computer using Windows, macOS/OSX or Linux.

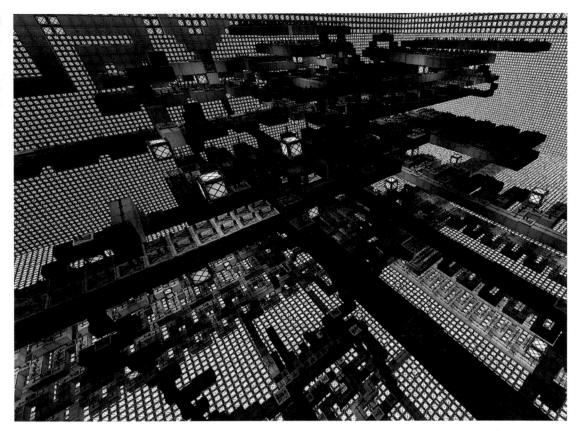

Redstone has transformed how players 'play' in Minecraft, allowing incredibly complex builds to be realised, such as this 'factory'.

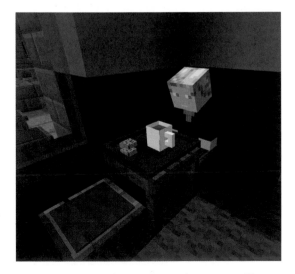

The introduction of non-player characters allows another dimension to be added to gameplay.

Fantastical projects have emerged from Minecraft's basic premise of mining and building a shelter.

ADVENTURE MODE

Adventures in Minecraft® are essentially games within the game, created by players for others to interact with. You can either download saved worlds or join other player's servers; one of the best resources for finding adventures to play is www.minecraftforum.net.

Although most players are familiar with Minecraft's Survival and Creative modes, you can also play Minecraft in Adventure mode. You can switch to Adventure mode from any other mode by opening the text window and entering the commands /gamemode adventure, /gamemode a or /gamemode 2.

Switching to Adventure mode limits some of the gameplay by not allowing the player to directly destroy blocks or place any blocks. The creator of the map can assign tools that can break certain blocks, and they can also use command blocks to create mechanisms that will trigger certain effects when the player interacts with particular blocks, but the player himself is limited to the map as it is intended to be played by the creator.

However, it's not necessary for you to change modes to play games created by other players: Adventure mode simply creates a tighter set of rules within which to experience someone else's creation. One of the best things about Minecraft is that there are no strict rules, so games and stories created by other players can be approached in a wide number of ways.

Adventure games cover a broad range of genres, but perhaps one of the most enduring is the creation of fantastical worlds and cities with a pseudo-historical basis, such as the distinctive *Emerald Heart* (left; pages 108–113) and *Kingdom of Lorlake* (this page; pages 222–227).

COMMAND BLOCK BASICS

When Minecraft® first appeared there were very few ways that builders could make a world in which another player could go on an adventure. Of course, that didn't stop people from finding ways to create their own games within the game. Mazes were one way to challenge other players, as they required no moving parts and could use stories relayed to the player on signs dotted around the labyrinth.

However, this changed as soon as redstone appeared in the game (see pages 22–23). In an instant an entire world of interactive electronics was born. Redstone gave players the ability to push buttons, open doors, lock things, make puzzles and even store data. The possibilities became unlimited…almost.

Even with redstone, there were still things that couldn't be done or that were very difficult to achieve. While builders

can be incredibly ingenious, the magic of Minecraft's tools is their accessibility, so to extend the abilities of redstone, command blocks were added to the game.

Command blocks are an extremely valuable resource in the world of interactive map making. Within each block, you can put a command. It's a sort of scripting language that you don't even have to leave Minecraft to use. You write the command right into the command block, activate it with some redstone, and it will run the command.

Command blocks can perform many different and amazing things, but you need to be aware that these are powerful tools. It's possible to crash your world, or turn every animal and monster in the game into a creeper, making it unplayable!

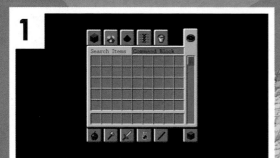

1 To create and change the way command blocks work you must be an operator (OP) on a server, or be in creative mode in your single player world. You won't find command blocks in your creative menu, so you will have to enter a command to start using them.

2 Open the chat window by pressing *t*, and then type: /give @p minecraft:command_ block. When you press the *Enter* you will run your first command and receive a single command block.

3

Place your command block on the ground. The direction a command block is facing can matter, so take note of the arrows on the block. With more than one command block, you can chain commands – but they need to have a direction so that they occur in order.

4

When you right-click the command block you can see a text field, as well as some other buttons. This is effectively what's happening 'inside' the command block and is where all the magic happens. Type /give @p minecraft:command_block and press 'Done'.

5

You will notice nothing happens! This is because the default state of a command block is that it is turned off: to activate it you need the power of redstone (refer to pages 22–23). Use a redstone block, torch, or button to power your command block (I like putting a button right on it).

6

When you power your command block, you will get another command block (the command you entered inside the command block at step 4 was to give you another command block). Now you can just press the button on your command block whenever you want another command block.

7

Let's have some fun with this. Open the command block interface again, and change the word 'command_block' to 'diamond'. Press 'Done' and power your command block again: just like magic, you now have a diamond!

8

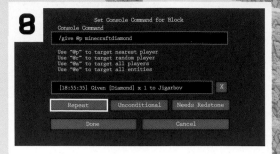

Open the interface one more time and press 'Impulse' until it says 'Repeat'. This makes the command repeat again and again while it is active.

9

When you press 'Done', notice that the command block has changed to blue. This is so you know that this is a repeating command block (although it isn't repeating yet).

10

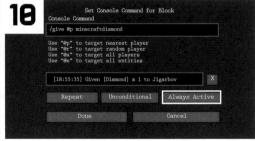

Open the command block and press 'Needs Redstone' until it displays 'Always Active'. This changes the command block so you don't even need to power it.

11

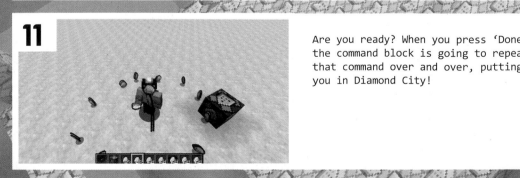

Are you ready? When you press 'Done', the command block is going to repeat that command over and over, putting you in Diamond City!

REDSTONE

One of the most interesting blocks in Minecraft® is redstone. Redstone can transmit power. In much the same way as an electrical wire, this means you can use redstone in circuits to operate mechanism components, such as doors, pistons and lamps, which can be activated using levers or buttons (in much the same way as an electrical circuit).

As well as being used to create wires, redstone dust can also create repeaters, which will strengthen the weakening signal that comes from increasing the length of the wires. Although using redstone is simpler than creating electric circuits in the real world, it still requires practice, and making mechanisms is something that will definitely take time to master. However, the results can be spectacular, allowing you to create anything from robots and computers to musical instruments and fully interactive games.

Throughout this book there are tutorials that will help you get to grips with this fundamental element, and on the page opposite we're going to look at a simple, but incredibly useful function for this versatile material: to open a door using a push button.

Redstone works in much the same way as electrical wire, allowing it to be used to connect various devices to create mechanisms.

1

Redstone appears as an item when you dig redstone ore – here you can see it as an item on the sandstone block. We've also placed an iron door opposite it, which is currently closed.

2

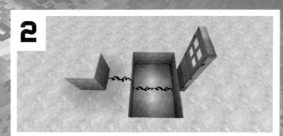

Use redstone dust to create a path from the point where you want to control the door (the sandstone block) to a block next to or under the door. This dust will power all the blocks it is pointing at or lying on.

3

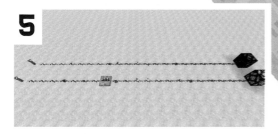

Place a button on the sandstone block and then press it. 'Power' travels through the redstone dust and into the block below the door. As soon as that block is powered, the door opens!

4

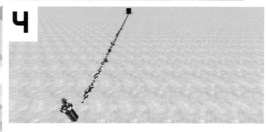

Redstone can be used for some amazing things, but it only travels for 15 blocks. Here, the redstone lamp at the top is too far from the redstone torch, so it won't turn on.

5

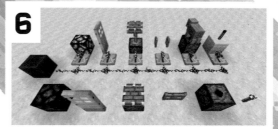

To overcome the limited distance you can add a repeater to the redstone 'wire', which makes the power run for another 15 blocks. In this example that's all that's needed to power the redstone lamp. Repeaters are made with redstone as well.

6

Redstone can be used to power all sorts of objects, including pistons, lamps, dispensers, gates and much more. Experiment to see what happens when you power things in your own Minecraft world!

MODS

Mods add content to Minecraft®, giving the player more ways to interact with their environment, changing gameplay or improving control. To improve the look of your worlds you can use texture packs, which can give blocks a more detailed look, and shaders, which change the lighting, smoothness and particle effects. This can have a dramatic effect on your map and fundamentally change how your world looks.

While texture packs and shaders can improve the look of your builds, editing tools such as WorldEdit, MCEdit and VoxelSniper will help with the build itself.

WorldEdit is an in-game tool that allows you to select, replace or delete thousands of blocks at a time. It can also be used to modify the randomly generated terrain, so you can flatten a mountain in an instant! It is particularly useful when you want to build a city, as it provides you with a way of copying and pasting whole areas, enabling an entire building to be replicated with the press of a button.

MCEdit is an open-source world editor that was originally developed to allow players to preserve builds created in older versions of Minecraft and move them into newer versions of the game. Updates to the editor now allow players to use a 'brush' tool to paint blocks into shapes, move spawn points and scale and export objects.

VoxelSniper enables terraforming on any scale, allowing players to create custom mountains, lakes, rivers, valleys and much more. Its strength is the detail-rich environments it can create, making it ideal for players looking to build intricate and precise maps that are packed with detail. However, it's definitely one for more experienced builders, and will only run on a server.

With each project in this book you'll find details of any mods used, so why not try some out for yourself?

Texture packs can transform the level of detail in your blocks, giving your Minecraft builds greater realism.

Shaders are one of the main ways in which you can inject atmosphere
into your builds, as they change the lighting in your world.

Plugins such as WorldEdit can help you with a variety of different
build tasks, ranging from terraforming to making domed roofs.

ADVENTURE GAME TIPS

This book contains lots of fantastic advice from some of the greatest Minecraft® mapmakers. These are the people behind the most popular and well-known Minecraft adventures, but these games didn't just happen by accident. No matter whether you are making a simple minigame or a sprawling, epic adventure, there are some general rules to follow if you plan on creating your own successful game within Minecraft.

APPEAL

Even if your game has a simple look and concept, you still have to make it exciting enough for people to want to play it. Creating an image directly from the game or producing a concept sketch that shows the player what to expect are both great ways of getting people interested. You could also give it a catchy, clever or mysterious name to draw players in.

LORE

Even with a basic minigame or maze, players want a reason 'why' they are doing what they are doing, so be sure to create some kind of story. Whether that means creating a theme around your minigames (having them set in a fairground, for example) or something that has to be retrieved from the centre of a maze, you should give players a context for what they are doing.

ACCESSIBILITY

You don't want players wandering around your map, not knowing what they should be doing or where they should be going. Make sure you give them the tools and information they need as soon as they start your game. Make it clear what they should be doing first and how to do it. Don't assume that every player will have played another game in the same genre before.

CHALLENGE

Even the simplest treasure hunt should have a little bit of a challenge involved. If you have designed the game to act as a tour around a beautiful structure you have made, simply putting things just out of reach or in clever places will help keep players engaged.

SATISFACTION

Player satisfaction isn't about them achieving the final goal of your game. Instead, it's about allowing the player to master the scenario in a way that challenges them just enough so they feel clever when they 'win'.

This means trying to anticipate the player's way of thinking and their behaviour. For example, most players would expect to find treasure behind a waterfall. They will look there for it because they just can't help it, but think how clever they will feel when they are rewarded (and how disappointed they will be if there's nothing there but water)!

REPLAY

If a player loves your game they will want to play it again, so give them a reason to come back. Whether it's to beat their highscore or to find another path or alternative ending, give them more to do the next time around. Also, don't forget this is Minecraft, so players will want to mess around with your rules and create their own way to play. They may try to make a game within your game, within the game of Minecraft. Let them!

Some of the most popular adventure games combine a gameplaying challenge with a strong storyline and stunning backdrops. That is certainly the case with *City of Love 2*, which you can see on pages 86–89.

GAME GUIDE

P34

P40

P46

P54

P60

P66

P72

P78

P86

P90

P96

P102

P108

P114

P120

P128

P134

P140

P146

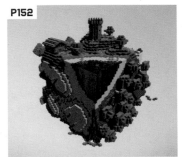

P152

P158

P164

P172

P180

P188

P190

P200

P206

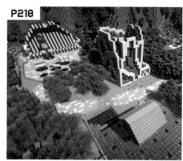
P210

P218

P222

P228

P232

P240

CHAPTER 1 UNFOLDING STORIES

COPS VS. ROBBERS

THE GAME

Cops vs. Robbers (or '*CvS*') tells the story of a dystopian world. Ruled by a corrupt police force that can do whatever it wants, people work as slaves in mines, where they have to farm huge amounts of gold to meet their everyday needs.

You can choose to play the game as a normal citizen, always obeying the 'cops', but the game will be pretty easy (and also a bit dull)! A greater challenge comes when you do something bad and have to defend yourself against an overwhelming number of cops. In doing so you will need to gather people to fight with you, plan your next move, learn about the city, and work out how you can use the environment to your advantage.

Cops vs. Robbers is a complete mod of the Minecraft® server, programmed using Java and complex redstone. In every new development there are a lot of mistakes that happen, and this one was no exception. It took six months to fix all the bugs and to prevent (or at least limit) cheating. It also took a while to balance the weapons used in the game: swords were initially far too strong, rocket launchers didn't harm anything and machine guns took way too long to fire!

THE BUILDER

Christian Uhl is a software engineer from Frankfurt, Germany, who is currently studying for a Masters degree in Computer Science. He first encountered Minecraft when he was working as a games magazine editor and was asked to test a new indie game. The developer – 'Notch' – gave him a press key, and a few days before the world was wowed by the game, Christian was playing Minecraft.

On the same day that the world found out about the game, Christian founded his own Minecrafting team ('Brauhaus der Hoffnung') and created a multiplayer server and forum. As one of the earliest German servers, a core team of leaders and builders quickly formed. However, Christian felt that the fun would stop if money became involved, so he never accepted any donations or payments.

Type of game: RPG
Difficulty: Easy or Hard
Time to play: Months

Number of players: 10–50
Shaders and mods used: Server specific
Time to build: Approx. 150 hours

AIRLOCK

If you plan to create a game where you can lock people up, you really need an airlock to prevent them breaking out of your cells. This method uses levers, but it could easily be built with pressure plates instead.

1

You will need a lot of wiring space, so dig a hole at least four blocks deep and six blocks wide, placing steel doors at each end. Make sure you can expand your hole downwards if you need more space.

2

Place a redstone torch on a stone below the doors to open them. Make sure you get the signal from the opening lever to the level below and wire them to the placed redstone torch.

3

Wire one lever to the redstone torch of one door. This door is directly controllable and should lead to the outside. Place three stones next to each other and wire the redstone torch to the left side as well.

4

Wire the second lever to the right side of the three stones. Make sure there is enough space between everything to prevent the redstone overlapping and creating a short circuit.

5

Place a redstone torch at the left and the right sides of the three blocks, and one redstone between them. This is the final NAND gate. If both redstone torches are powered, the output signal is off.

6

In case your signal from the opener is inverted, you need to add one NOT gate to your wiring (a regular powered redstone torch).

7

Wire the NAND gate to the other door.

8

Trigger the openers. Only one door should be open at a time – if something is wrong, check the redstone cables.

9

Because the hole is four blocks deep, you can easily place any block above it without breaking the redstone cables.

10

You can use iron bars to create a cell on one side of your airlock, and you can also build a whole cell complex behind it.

CHRISTIAN'S TIPS

TIP 1

Start with a public beta test as soon as possible, as people will find mistakes in places you would never think to look. If you know some cheaters, ask them to play it too – only cheaters are willing to do a triple wall base duck lag jump 200 times just to skip one level!

TIP 2

Never plan too big. Start with the smallest possible setup and continue developing it until you've got it working. Then continue adding more features or levels.

TIP 3

Never plan on doing everything yourself. It will motivate you to complete your build if other people are helping.

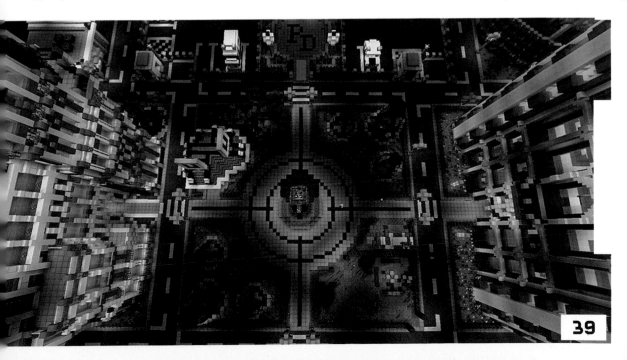

THE DOCTOR

THE GAME

The Doctor is a map created for roleplayers, which is available for public download. As the map was created with the intention of having a player roleplay within it, it was designed with as much attention to detail as possible; the hospital has surgery rooms, wards, a canteen, elevators and even a library, so there can be plenty of scenarios for players to take on.

The map was originally created for 'CibSeption' and 'Gizzy14gazza', two well-known Minecraft® YouTube roleplayers, and the idea was simply to create a hospital. However, the project quickly expanded and eventually turned into a whole city filled with secrets and areas to explore.

THE BUILDER

Co-founded by 'Janakin' and Nikolaj Anderson in 2013, Sunfury is a team that mostly focuses on making minigames, although it also likes to create complex scenarios such as *The Doctor*.

Janakin says he gets his inspiration from random things (sometimes it's just a shape he sees somewhere), while Nikolaj cites his father and brother as influences on his gaming life. Having great imaginations has meant that both they and their team have been able to create some of Minecraft's most original and popular games.

Type of game: RPG
Difficulty: Easy
Time to play: 20 hours

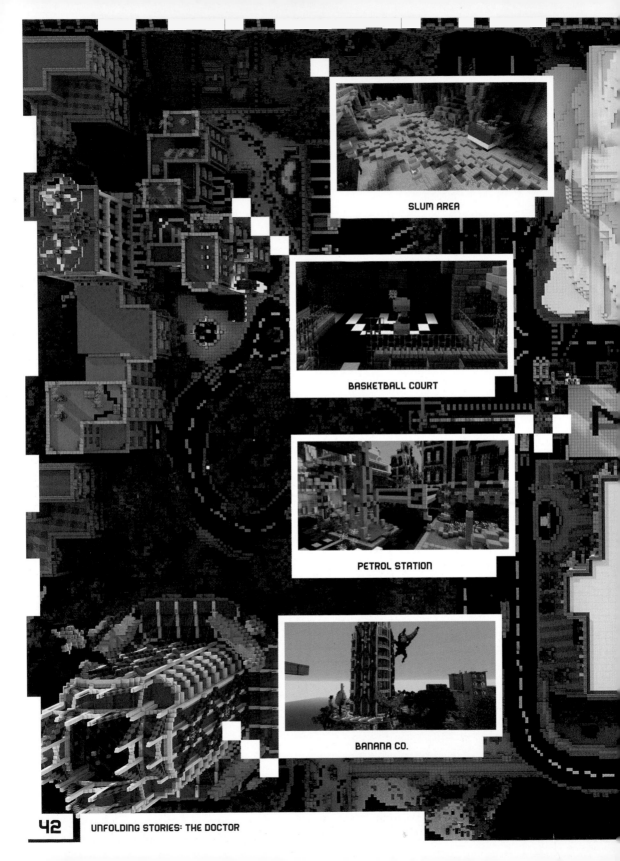

SLUM AREA

BASKETBALL COURT

PETROL STATION

BANANA CO.

DOCTORS' OFFICES

HARBOUR BRIDGE

SUBMARINE

The Doctor started with a hospital (top), but grew into a city containing plenty of detail-rich areas to explore (centre). This includes a petrol station (bottom), which consists mainly of iron blocks, with coloured wool forming its red and green logo.

The doctors' offices are constructed from quartz and have very light colours. A yellow line on the wall works as a colour code for that section of the hospital (top), while other sections of the building use different colours (centre and bottom).

45

THE BEEHIVE

THE GAME

The Beehive is a giant creation, featuring numerous machines and warfare vehicles, packed into a backyard beehive setting. Led by Corbin Rainbolt and Jason King, and with input from many goCreative members, *The Beehive* provides an immersive experience for players of all ages.

The general theme is 'bees versus ants', with the ants attacking the beehive and the bees needing to protect it. There is a deeper meaning, though, which is about how humans treat bees, with pesticides killing them off in a way that may well backfire spectacularly on humanity. The game was used to help promote 'The Bee Cause', which supports caring for the United Kingdom's bee population.

The team began building the hive from the outside and then added the machines, vehicles and many hidden 'Easter eggs', such as characters from the movie, *Monsters University*. However, the most spectacular feature is undoubtedly the Queen Bee.

THE BUILDER

goCreative is a team of talented content creators specialising in Minecraft® builds for businesses, charities and other organisations. The team formed in February 2014, was reshuffled in 2015, and now consists of 30 members from 12 different countries who come together to use Minecraft as a marketing, educational and gaming tool.

The Minecraft community is extremely important to the team. All its members originate from the wider Minecraft world and were picked with care to ensure they could work with each other in small groups.

The goCreative team is always pushing the boundaries of Minecraft and likes to venture out into other areas as well, such as graphic design and its own Minecraft-oriented social sharing site, Block Arts. The members also give regular talks about their work at business events.

Type of game: Story
Difficulty: Easy
Time to play: 1 hour+

Number of players: Unlimited
Time to build: 700 hours

ANT

For this tutorial we're going to build one of the attacking ants. However, to speed up the build process we'll only build one half of the ant, which can then be mirrored over to the other side. This is a great time-saver!

1

Make a layout frame measuring 28x22. Then, use grey hardened clay to create half a sphere with a radius of four blocks from the centre of the right side. Add a few extra blocks to turn the sphere into an oval.

2

This shows how the back of the ant should look. It is effectively cut in half, so the flat side is the centre of the ant; eventually you will mirror everything to get the full ant.

3

Use soul sand to create another sphere to the left of the ant's back, this time with a radius of three blocks. Again, turn it into an oval shape, as described previously.

4

To create the ant's neck add a third, smaller sphere with a radius of two blocks, then add a few blocks underneath to make it longer. Use red hardened clay for this.

5

Use red wool to create the head, making it the same shape as the neck. Add a 'nose' at the bottom front and cut a small hole into the side for an eye. Add three coal blocks to the back of the hole (in the shape of a reversed 'L') and a dragon egg.

6

For the antenna, use brown wool, curving it towards the front of the ant.

7

Create the ant's 'shoulders' by adding a couple of granite blocks diagonally up the back and centre part of the ant as shown.

8

Now you can add the connection between the shoulders and the legs, using three different blocks that arch out towards you. Have the rear joint bend to the right and the front one bend towards the left.

9

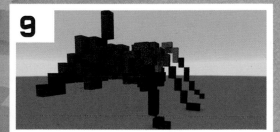

Add legs using red nether brick, built at a slight angle down towards the ground. Add a few horizontal blocks at the bottom of the leg to create a tiny foot. For a mouth you can add five blocks: two on top and three below.

10

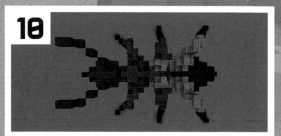

You will now have completed one half of the ant, so it's time to mirror it over to the other half, as shown here. You can do this manually, or use various plugins to duplicate your build, but don't mirror the centre line.

With its intriguing blend of bugs and technology, *The Beehive* is one of the most unique builds goCreative has ever created.

Although the game is based on the premise of 'bees versus ants', *The Beehive* also has a deeper meaning to it, about how man is impacting on his environment.

TEMATOS

THE GAME

Known as 'Achiminecraft' in the Minecraft®
community, Achi's main project – which he has been
working on for years – is creating a cinematic
adventure within Minecraft called *Acanacati*. *Tematos*
is the spectacular second chapter of this adventure,
which takes its inspiration from Japanese roleplaying
games, such as *Final Fantasy*.

Achi started by creating a miniature of his design in
Minecraft, based on a sketch. He worked from that
to create the palace, building out from the centre with
paths returning to the middle. He is now working on
the city that will feature in the third chapter of his
epic video series, but in the meantime you can see
Tematos at https://youtu.be/3I3I11PFiBs.

THE BUILDER

Achi is a musician from Japan who likes to make
cinematic videos that combine his love of Minecraft
and music. Like many builders, he was encouraged
by friends to try the game to start with. Although
he began playing in Survival mode, it was the
creative community that really inspired him to
experiment with the game.

From a very young age it has been Achi's ambition
to work in the games industry. As he's developed his
interest he has specialised more and more in music
and would ultimately like to be a game composer.

Type of game: Cinematic adventure
Mods: Minecraft Forge, OptiFine,
GLSL Shaders MOD, Camera Studio,
LotMetaBlockPack, Better Grass
& Leaves Mod, Better Foliage,
MinecraftIM, IntelliInput,
LiteLoader, VoxelMap, DaFlight,
WorldEditWrapper, Macro/Keybind mod,
WorldEditCUI, Custom NPCs, UgoCraft,
HariboteAirCraft, Minema, Mineshot

Shaders: KUDA Shaders, Sonic
Ether's Unbelievable Shaders,
Continuum Shaders
Plugins: WorldEdit, WorldGuard,
VoxelSniper, TSP_A_Jumper, TSP_A_
MetaDataChanger, TSP_A_Replacer,
TSP_A_RotateInventoryLine,
TSP_A_WeatherController, TSP_A_
EasySelectPainting, ToggleInventory,
Build Commands, BiomeEdit, MetaCycler,
AutoSaveWorld, Dynmap, ExtendHotBar
Time to build: 1¼ years

Breathtaking opening cinematic scenes typify Japanese roleplaying games, and with its stunning landscape *Tematos* is no exception.

In the video an airship flies over elaborate cities and castles. It is attacked by a giant, flying dragon-like creature, which is ultimately stopped in its tracks by a huge force field.

SUNARIS

THE GAME

Sunaris is an adventure game created with a variety of custom-built areas. It features a dense, mysterious jungle with thick trees, which leads to a large canyon. Within this is the entrance to a temple, inside which you will discover long passageways leading into multiple chambers. At the end is a great hall where a giant samurai statue watches over the altar.

Inspired in part by adventure movies such as *Indiana Jones*, a lot of research went into the *Sunaris* map, which included studying the architecture of traditional Japanese temples. This resulted in a map containing many curved lines, which is clearly difficult to reproduce in such a blocky environment.

THE BUILDER

Nikolaj Anderson comes from Denmark, where he manages and coordinates all of the mapmaking for the Sunfury team. Nikolaj has been playing Minecraft® for over four years, but he was far from impressed when he first set eyes on the game. His first playing experience produced a horrible-looking house made entirely from cobblestone, but as he had played for 20 hours straight, he knew this was a game to be reckoned with.

The real hook for Nikolaj has been the community, and the recognition he has gained with his team. His focus is now on the management side of things, which can prove just as challenging and satisfying as building. With the Sunfury team, Nikolaj has to do some serious coordinating to make sure that everyone gets to contribute to the final product and uses their best skills and experience.

On any given project Nikolaj will have to talk with a number of specialist builders. This often results in an absurd amount of documents for textures, gameplay mechanics, buildings, features created through command block magic and so on!

Type of game: Adventure
Difficulty: Easy
Time to play: 30 minutes

Number of players: Multiplayer
Shaders and mods used: VoxelSniper, WorldEdit
Time to build: 2 weeks

UNFOLDING STORIES

INTEGRATION

Sunaris offers a variety of different areas, which required various materials to create. With dense jungle, a temple, corridors and rooms, this type of map can be complicated to put together, so let's look at how you can integrate disparate parts into a single adventure:

- Build up a rough terraforming layout. In *Sunaris* there needed to be a small cave that opened up to a large open canyon, where people could admire some extensive, jungle-themed terraforming.

- Use VoxelSniper brushes to shape the terrain, and then use WorldEdit brushes to paint colours into the terrain and add grass. With *Sunaris*, all the trees were built by hand to give a chaotic jungle feel.

- The interior of the temple starts with a long corridor with pillars for players to jump across, and a perilous drop below. At the end of the corridor is the main hall, which is the grandest part of the map. A great way to tackle a build like this is to create small sections and use WorldEdit to copy and paste them to form the rough shape of a larger room.

- One of the most time-consuming parts of the process is making sure all the areas that have been copied in fit together. This could mean adding some more detail to the walls, or using glowstone to create patterns in water. With *Sunaris*, overgrown walkways were used to link the various chambers and allow the player to travel between sections.

- You may want to add functionality to your adventure map. This map was used as a set in an animation by the YouTube animation channel Hyperdream Studios, and also featured as a pod-racing map thanks to the additional use of command blocks and mine carts.

Integrate the structure into its surroundings. Using leaves, grass and breaking open some parts of the structure can enhance the ruined feel of your temple and make it seem as though it has been lost in time.

Although building *Sunaris* involved researching ancient temple architecture,
the map was also inspired by classic adventure movies.

ERONEV MANSION ADVENTURE

THE GAME

Eronev Mansion Adventure was one of the first Minecraft® maps to gain a lot of public attention. Its multiple endings, exploration aspects and deep story meant it could be replayed many times over, and this set it apart from a lot of the other maps that were available at the time.

This adventure map is in the style of a 'Metroidvania game', where you are granted upgrades to your abilities so you can find and access new areas. It's strongly influenced by the classic game, *The Legend of Zelda*, and its builder, Tim Gehrig (aka 'Jigarbov'), hoped to capture a similar air of adventure – his favourite games are those where the story twists and turns and always gives you something new to see or do.

The game itself is quite easy, as the focus is mainly on the story and progressing your character, with plenty of exploration opportunities as you wander around the environment. There is a lot of freedom in how you experience the game: if you want to speed through to the ending you can do so in 30 minutes, but if you want to explore and take your time it can take several hours.

For Jigarbov, the process for building any map is extremely haphazard. He often begins with a glimmer of an idea and then starts placing blocks, allowing the build to grow organically. With this adventure map he found a beautiful landscape matching the one he had imagined, and then built a mansion into the hillside. After this, the village flowed down into the world and different characters came into being. He wanted to have lots of locations, so a significant amount of world modification was carried out, including creating a huge glacier, terraforming a desert, and building alternate versions of the village that were used for the end sequences. He says the story was quite generic at first, but as the characters formed in the world, the protagonist began to write himself.

Type of game: Story
Difficulty: Easy
Time to play: 1-3 hours

Number of players: 1-4
Shaders and mods used: MCEdit, INVedit
Time to build: 200 hours

THE BUILDER

Jigarbov is an Australian mapmaker, who now lives in Canada. He enjoys travelling and seeing the world, and this has equipped him with experiences that he applies to his Minecraft® adventure maps.

Originally, Jigarbov's interest in Minecraft lay in its survival aspect, but it didn't take long for him to see the potential it had as a gaming platform. Adventure maps have become Jigarbov's favourite things to build, but he admits that it's fairly selfish – for him it's all about having fun while he builds, and then getting further enjoyment from watching people having to deal with the situations he's put them in. The great thing about making these kinds of maps is there are plenty of people making YouTube videos about them, so Jigarbov can watch lots of different people playing his maps!

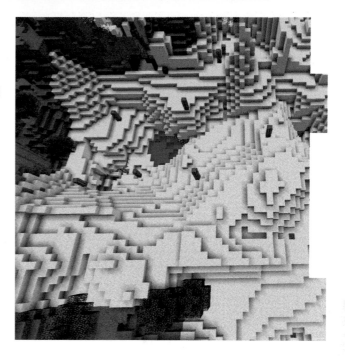

JIGARBOV'S TIPS

TIP 1

There is no wrong way to make a map. Some people are highly organised and have everything planned out ahead of time. This makes the actual build easy and streamlined, but it can lack organic growth.

TIP 2

If being organised doesn't work for you then build by the seat of your pants! Putting pieces into the world and reacting to them, and writing the non-player characters after the build is complete can make the world feel more fluid and 'natural'.

TIP 3

If neither of these methods works for you, maybe combine them? Plan some parts, but work organically with others – by creating a synergy between the two you might come up with something very special!

The *Eronev Mansion Adventure* map has plenty of places for you to explore, letting you choose the pace at which you experience – and complete – the game.

UNFOLDING STORIES: ERONEV MANSION ADVENTURE

THE ASYLUM

THE GAME

The Asylum is an atmospheric, story-driven horror map based on a person who crashes their car and is looking for somewhere to make a phone call to reach help. Unfortunately the place they find is the abandoned Chartham Asylum, which is haunted by its former residents!

The map is easy and offers multiple-choice scenarios. However, while it only takes around 15 minutes to play, it has plenty of jump scares, a very creepy atmosphere and a big twist in the storyline! Some areas can be missed out entirely, making it even quicker to play, but exploring the map as fully as possible will make for a much more fun experience.

Sunfury originally built *The Asylum* in 2013, but it wasn't until 2015 that the team decided to make a full game out of the map. In the process, the team revamped large areas that had become outdated and enlisted the help of three players who work heavily with command blocks: 'Octavigon', 'TypicalPixels', and 'iReapism'. Sunfury then recruited 'Monsterfish' to help create some textures, while 'themineman23', 'Stervma' and Janakin created the storyline so the command blockers had some guidelines to work to.

The team was happy with the outcome of its creation, but with a Halloween deadline, some features didn't make it into the final game. This has left Sunfury with plans for future games, some of which it is already hard at work on – although the team isn't sharing details just yet!

Type of game: Story
Difficulty: Easy
Time to play: 15 minutes

Number of players: 1
Shaders and mods used: None
Time to build: Approx. 150 hours

THE BUILDER

Founded by Janakin in 2013, Sunfury is a team with members who have quite different talents and personalities, but who work well together to create games that have garnered them a strong reputation. As well as games, structures and scenarios, the team also creates for YouTubers, and builds for the animation team Hyperdream Studios.

As the mapmaking community has evolved over the years, Sunfury has changed along with it, creating ever more complex games and maps. Spurred on by the ambitious ideas of the wider community, the team appreciates the sense of competition and encouragement that comes from everyone working on bigger and better ideas with every new creation.

Despite being quite different from one another, the individual team members share a passion for Minecraft® and a desire to make a name for themselves. Through Sunfury they can bring their designs to life with redstone to create games.

SUNFURY'S TIPS

TIP 1

If you're working as part of a team, it's important to keep your command blocks neatly organised and labelled. This will help other command blockers working on a project when they look at your setup.

TIP 2

Make organised documents that everyone involved has access to. Sunfury uses Google Docs to make documents for every aspect of the project, whether it's texture-, command block-, story-, or building-related.

TIP 3

Don't take on too big a project if you don't have the team for it. Start small and push yourself – it's far better to finish the project than put hours into something that you can't be bothered finishing.

CRAFTING A STORY

The Asylum uses some of the latest techniques within mapmaking. When it was created it was truly revolutionary, as it includes voice acting, high-end builds, redstone, cutscenes, custom sounds, custom textures and a creepy storyline with a twist. Let's look at the technical aspects of creating the game:

- When creating the story for *The Asylum*, the team wanted a spooky theme relating to Halloween. It is important to have a strong story with a good twist at the end to leave the player wanting more – it could even make them want to play the game again!

- With the storyline in place you need to build a map around it. Sunfury built a large, empty asylum building, which was filled with random corridors that were unrelated to the building's layout. This immediately had a disorienting effect on the player.

- Using a custom resource pack can be extremely effective if done correctly. In *The Asylum* there are multiple custom sound effects, including screams, narrative speech for the player, character interactions and creepy background noises, such as door slams and laughter.

- Sunfury wanted the player to be walking slower than normal (and without the ability to jump) to add tension to the player experience. To add a long-lasting effect such as this you will need to use the /effect command.

Inventory search can be used for many things, but in *The Asylum* it's primarily used for keys to unlock different sectors of the map. When the player picks up a key, a command block registers it in the player's inventory, which makes it possible to determine whether the player can open a locked door when they walk over to it.

- One of the most challenging parts of *The Asylum* is a cutscene at the start. To create the effect of a tree being hit by lightning and crashing down on to the road, Sunfury used the /clone command to reset and change the scenario from the road being intact to being blocked by the destroyed tree.

- The functionality of *The Asylum* relies on a large amount of redstone and command block logic. When the player is exploring the map, certain events that happen are achieved using a radius search with a constant redstone clock connected to the command block, checking if the condition has been met.

- The WorldEdit plugin allows you to set an area of blocks and customise it in a variety of ways, including copying and pasting. This can also be achieved using command blocks. For example, at one point in *The Asylum*, the environment changes to block off a path and direct the player in another direction.

- All the cutscenes in the map were created using armour stand 'stop-motion' animation. This involves using long chains of command blocks with a new armour stand position update command in each one. By updating the position rapidly and moving the armour stand a little at a time, you can create an impression of motion.

Mobs can be very useful in Minecraft® horror minigames, and several are used in *The Asylum*. For example, they are used for a stage of the map where a zombie runs towards the player with particles flying around it, making it seem like a dark spirit.

CITY OF LOVE

THE GAME

With *City of Love*, Jigarbov's goal was to create a dating sim within Minecraft®. This wasn't something that had been tried before, so there were a number of major challenges involved in manipulating the game's engine to do what was needed.

In the game, the player is living in an urban environment and desperately wants to find love. To enable this there needed to be a multitude of characters and the world had to change around the player as they completed dates with each of them. In total there are eight characters, each exhibiting branching dialogue patterns that react to your responses while conversations are taking place. One of Jigarbov's favourite characters is Amy, a happy-go-lucky girl who enjoys the company of cats. There is a lot more to her, of course, but we don't want to spoil the surprise!

As the team was aiming for a level of realism, the characters were written to be believable (albeit with some extremely exaggerated flaws that sometimes don't come to light until it is too late). There is a lot of comedy involved in those surprises, which makes 'let's play' videos dynamic and reactive; *City of Love* is perfect YouTube material, as the huge number of videos of this map proves.

The map itself is very easy, as it's almost impossible to die – the focus is based primarily on interactions with different characters and the world around you. Because of its non-linear nature, people have often referred to *City of Love* as a sandbox title (see page 14). However, while that is true to a certain extent, there aren't a lot of other activities outside the direct interactions with the cast.

Because of the things the build group wanted to do with *City of Love*, a whole new way of thinking about custom maps was needed. In the past, stories had been linear and there were usually only one or two main characters, plus a huge assortment of other characters designed only to guide you on your quest. Here, however, Jigarbov wanted to focus on the personality of each character and make sure

Type of game: Adventure/Dating sim
Difficulty: Easy
Time to play: 1–3 hours
Number of players: 1

Minecraft version: 1.6 (only works with Minecraft 1.6; players must downgrade their client if necessary)
Shaders and mods used: MCEdit, TexelElf's filters
Time to build: 450 hours

they felt unique. To help with this, each of the main contributors to the map was tasked with creating the personality of one or two characters. In some cases their original creator would write the character in his or her (or its!) entirety, but in other instances Jigarbov would finish them off based on what he thought the character would do.

It's the thoughtfulness of how the characters are drawn that makes the cast so diverse: there are three men, three women, one robot and a transgender character. The team felt it was important there weren't any limits on the player's interactions, so the characters ignore the gender of the player. This means the player has free reign to choose whomever they like best, without any assumptions made based on their own gender.

City of Love was a pioneering game in Minecraft® and it remains unusual to this day. Even now – three years after its release – there are very few games that contain branching dialogue. Such is its popularity that Jigarbov is making a sequel. You can get a sneak peek at *City of Love 2* on the following pages.

THE BUILDER

Jigarbov is a well-known Minecraft game maker who has made single-player adventures, linear stories and large-scale multiplayer adventures, as well as working on huge collaborations. However, it was becoming increasingly difficult to find something new and fresh, until he came up with a brilliant idea for a silly little conversation game.

Jigarbov's friends were discussing ways to have a dynamic conversation in Minecraft when he had the idea to use scoreboards to count through a dialogue tree. The player's inputs would work their way through the tree to create the talk-and-response system Jigarbov's group imagined.

The team behind this map was a group of Jigarbov's Minecraft friends, including 'Faume', 'Nirgalbunny', and 'SirVladimyr'. Nirgalbunny came up with the original prototype, and from there a strong system was created and implemented in the game. Working with these friends not only made it easy to share ideas, but also encouraged the team to work hard when the going was tough.

When it appeared, *City of Love* was Minecraft's first dating sim, combining a strong storyline with a distinct level of humour and realism.

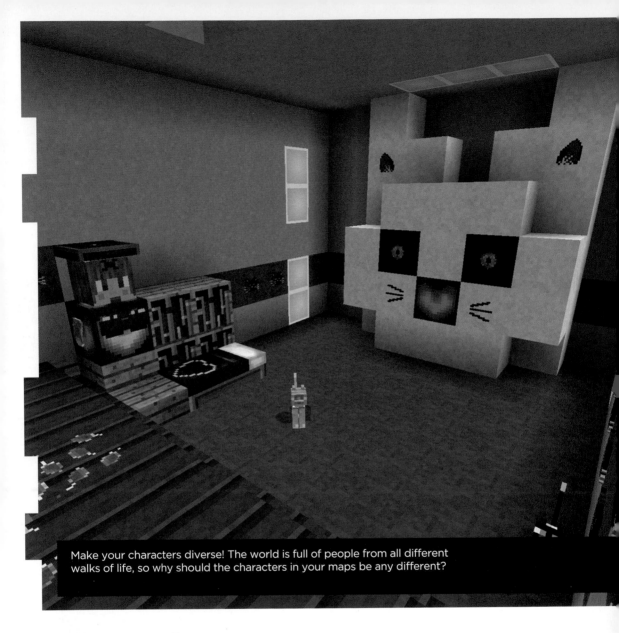

Make your characters diverse! The world is full of people from all different walks of life, so why should the characters in your maps be any different?

JIGARBOV'S TIPS

TIP 1

Play with your writing style so that your characters don't all sound the same. Let other people help you; they can offer valuable differences in perspective.

TIP 2

Try to make your world feel alive! Have each character interact with the world around them; sub characters should interact realistically with the main characters!

Jigarbov's ambitious map required plenty of unique locations for the player to explore, as well as numerous non-player characters to help bring the world to life.

PLAYER SKINS

Something *City of Love* does well is put the player in a world filled with life. There are a few ways to achieve this, but having plenty of non-player characters (NPCs) is a great option. Luckily, Minecraft® has something called a 'player skull', which searches the Minecraft servers for other people's skins. This lets you create hundreds of unique characters without having to do any of the hard work!

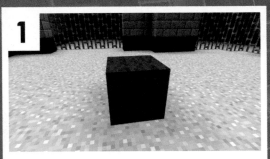

1

Place the body first. For this walkthrough we've made it a simple block.

2

In the creative menu you can find some monster player heads such as the zombie skull. If you put that on a green block you have yourself a zombie!

3

Throw a sign on and your zombie is an NPC!

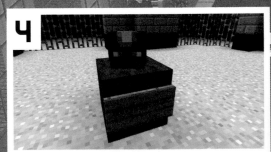

4

Too simple? Put this command in your console in creative mode: /give @p skull 1 3 {SkullOwner:Jigarbov} Now you have Jigarbov's head to use as an NPC character!

5

You can put all your friends in too, just change the command from Jigarbov to someone else you know.

6

If you want to get a bit more technical, get an armour stand and a set of armour (you can put all the armour on the stand just by right clicking it).

Put on the head and you'll have a slightly more anatomically correct NPC.

To get even more technical, summon an armour stand using this command:
/summon ArmourStand ~ ~ ~
{NoBasePlate:1b,ShowArms:1b}

9

Dress up your new-and-improved armour stand and he or she will really look the part.

10

You can also pose armour stands. An easy way of doing this is to use Lars Martens's online armour stand poser at www.haselkern.com.

CITY OF LOVE 2

THE GAME

City of Love 2 is a direct sequel to Jigarbov's original Minecraft® dating sim, *City of Love*. Like the original, the sequel continues to combine themes of love and humour; you get to know characters through a series of conversations and activities, and can even get them to like you enough to marry you!

This time around, the game is more sophisticated. In the original version, the dialogue trees were rudimentary, characters moved around by way of a floating head in a mine cart, and all the dialogue was delivered as text in the chat window with the player's responses limited to 'red' (no, bad, disagree) and 'green' (yes, good, agree). Now, articulated block models represent each character and they can follow the player, rather than being limited to static, predetermined paths. The characters also have voice-acted dialogue and the reply options have much greater depth.

Although *City of Love 2* is still in development, the goal is to make it easy to enjoy, but hard enough for those who are looking for a challenge. What made the first game so special was that people of all skill levels could enjoy it and that carries over to this game. However, each minute of added gameplay takes a lot longer to create than it used to – there aren't many Minecraft maps that have voice acting, or have the player watch cinematic conversations play out with other characters in the world.

THE BUILDER

Having been an active part of the Minecraft community for over six years, Jigarbov has seen it go through many versions, with different groups of people and different generations of creators and content makers. For this map, he pulled together many of his friends from past projects, including the Broken Buttons team that he's worked with previously. Jigarbov would name-check everyone involved, but with the map still in development and new people helping all the time, it's hard to know who else could play a part!

Type of game: Adventure/Dating sim
Difficulty: Easy
Time to play: 1–4 hours
Number of players: 1

Minecraft version: 1.10
Shaders and mods used: MCEdit,
TexelElf's filters, BDCraft Cubik
Time to build: 1000 hours

JIGARBOV'S TIPS

TIP 1

As technology increases, the mapmaking workload grows, so make sure you have plenty of time to do the things you want or need to do. The same map made five years ago would take significantly less time to build because there were fewer things you could do with Minecraft® back then!

TIP 2

Make your systems as modular and as flexible as possible. If you can retrofit all of your systems with different types of content it will make the whole creation system easier.

In *City of Love 2*, for example, every conversation is made using the same dialogue system, which makes adding a new conversation very easy.

TIP 3

When it comes to voice acting, try to get people who match the character you're writing for or find someone who can change their voice. Poor voice acting can ruin the player's experience.

As the sequel to an already popular game, Jigarbov knew that *City of Love 2* needed to be bigger and better in every way. The build has already seen him and his ever-growing team invest more than 1000 hours in it, with more work still to come.

SYMBIOSIS

THE GAME

Symbiosis depicts a struggle between Nature and parasites that have come from a deep, unexplored part of space. The map is primarily story driven and atmospheric, so there is little difficulty to it from the player's perspective, but it was still quite a challenging project to create.

The build was started by 'Denzarou' and 'Echto' of the Everbloom Studios team, but many of the team's members were busy, so they didn't have the time to contribute majorly to the project. However, there were a few people who spent many sleepless nights labouring to get the map out, including Isaac. As far as he's concerned, the best thing about the map is how the elements blend together to make an organic battleground; he's really proud of what the team managed to create, especially considering their lack of time and resources.

THE BUILDER

Isaac is from Pasadena, California, and is a member and builder for Everbloom Studios. He discovered Minecraft® when he was 11 and found a very small server where he would watch people create amazing things. Isaac would then try to figure out how they could do such complex things with blocks and attempt to mimic them using his own personal taste and creativity.

When he started out, there were very few people on the game, but Isaac was drawn to the idea of working with friends on various projects. He met people on small creative servers and would enjoy taking a break from life to mess around with them in Minecraft. Six years on, he still enjoys building with friends, which is exactly what he has found with Everbloom Studios.

Type of game: Story/Exploration
Number of players: 1
Time to play: 1-2 hours

PARASITE

This build demonstrates how to make one of the robotic parasites that can be found in *Symbiosis*. The process involves some organics skill, so it may be a little challenging to complete.

1

Start by creating the parasite's core. This can be made of a bright colour such as red, green or blue.

2

Build a space between the core and the front of the parasite to add depth to its body.

3

Add a light stone cap at the front of the space and then build up a proboscis. Make sure it gets thinner as you reach the end.

4

Create some dark rings to act as sockets to build claws out from.

5

Build out some claws at the front of the parasite; these will allow it to lock on to its target.

6

Next, add a spiral pattern to the main core to give the parasite some detail.

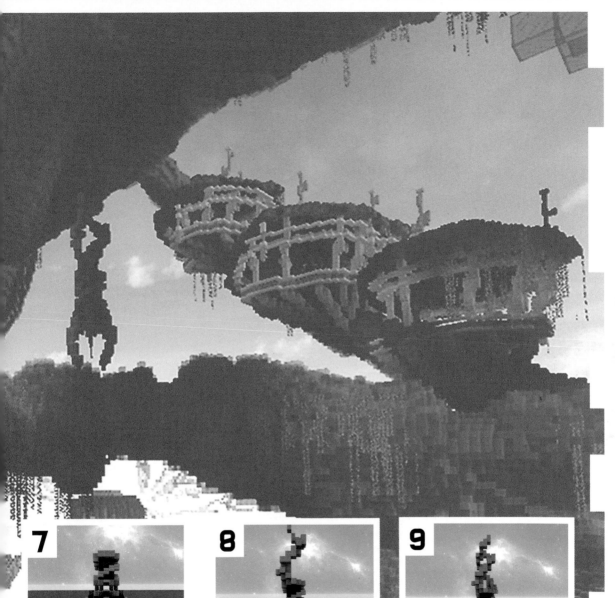

7

Place a spacer on top of the core to give you a level platform to work on when you build the parasite's tail.

8

As you build upwards, keep a constant gradient while working around a circle set out by your spacer. This will give you the spiral design you are looking for.

9

Repeat the previous step on the opposite side of the parasite to finish the build.

UNFOLDING STORIES: SYMBIOSIS

Depicting a war between Nature and alien parasites involved both organic and robotic elements. The challenge was blending these two distinctly different design elements.

JUNKYARD WARFARE

THE GAME

Junkyard Warfare is a monumental creation based
on the conflict between a pack of hounds and a horde
of barbaric outcasts, as they compete for water in a
dried-up wasteland. Managers Florian Funke and
Jason King led the creation, with input from the
entire goCreative team to conjure a visually stunning
atmosphere for Minecrafters to enjoy.

The purpose of the map was to provide an in-game
experience like no other, which goCreative tried to
achieve by setting up a server that anyone can join.
The game features in-game cinematics and some
special customisations that make exploring the
map easier.

The style of *Junkyard Warfare* combines recycling
and junk to create a visually spectacular adventure
map that features multiple areas and items to
explore, including a portal, a giant house, cars
and containers, spread across a map covering
2000x2000 blocks!

THE BUILDER

Florian Funke comes from Herford, Germany.
While he was at school he co-founded goCreative
with Brandon Relph, and what started as a hobby
has now become a full-time career. Florian and
Brandon (now joint CEOs of the company) have
turned goCreative into a serious business that takes
on all kinds of commissioned Minecraft® builds.

Type of game: Story
Difficulty: Easy
Time to play: 1 hour+

Number of players: Unlimited
Time to build: 400 hours

UNFOLDING STORIES

The goCreative team started the *Junkyard Warfare* build with the main fortress and worked outward, adding more and more detail along the way.

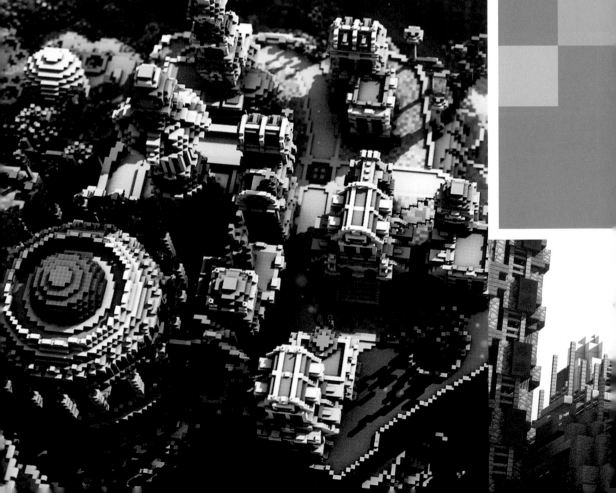

CHAPTER 2 **PARKOUR AND ROLLERCOASTERS**

SPAGHETTI ROLLERCOASTER

THE GAME

Spaghetti Rollercoaster is a whole-island amusement park. Although it is designed as a place for visitors who want good entertainment, there are also homes for the park workers, so everywhere you look you can see steampunk houses releasing clouds of white steam.

As the map was created for a rollercoaster contest, the main attraction is a crazy rollercoaster. You can ride around the island by cart, but to add some interaction the builder, Daniel, invented a gameplay element: you get a bow and your target is to shoot buttons placed on red wool. Like most carnival games, it sounds easy, but it's actually quite challenging!

Although it looks complicated, creating the huge Ferris wheel at the centre of the island was the easiest and fastest part of Daniel's build. He placed it on top of the mountain so it would be visible from almost any angle. Dotting various houses around was a relatively straightforward exercise, while the least fun part was creating the railway.

Daniel admits that despite its spectacular look, *Spaghetti Rollercoaster* is one of his least-favourite creations. The problem for him is that building for competitions means you usually have a very limited time to work on an idea. So, while it might all look fine from a visitor's perspective, from a builder's perspective there can be a lot of unfinished parts.

THE BUILDER

Daniel is from Jawor, Poland, and was introduced to Minecraft® by a friend. Since then he has been creating his own fantasy worlds and has also worked as part of a few build teams. For him, the greatest appeal of the game is the ability to create his own world with his own rules, enabling him to construct a dream version of 'life'.

Type of game: Adventure
Difficulty: Easy
Time to play: Minutes
Number of players: 1

Minecraft version: Up to 1.7
Shaders and mods used: Sonic Ether's
Unbelievable Shaders (SEUS), MCEdit
Time to build: 20 hours

**PARKOUR AND
ROLLERCOASTERS**

STEAMPUNK WAREHOUSE

This tutorial is for a simple, but attractive, steampunk warehouse, like those found in Daniel's *Spaghetti Rollercoaster* map. The design is flexible, so you can really make this building your own; you could add more floors, for example, or double the size of everything to make it larger.

1

Using wooden planks, build a 2x2x1 square. At the corners of the square place dark logs. One level higher than this lay dark logs to create the perimeter of a square, without corners.

2

Fill the square you created in step 1 with wooden planks to make a floor. Put stone brick slabs at the corners. On top of these use dark logs to build three-block high corners for the walls.

3

Add the roof. On both flanks of the warehouse use stone stairs to create the lower edge of the roof, which should span the upright logs.

4

Set stairs upside down to connect the lower edges you added in the previous step. On top of each stair place a stone brick block (indicated by red wool here). Repeat this to create a frame at both ends of the structure.

5

Fill in the roof with dark wooden planks. Use dark wooden plank stairs to line up with the stone stairs, and a line of dark wooden planks where there is a stone brick block (again, shown in red here).

6

Create walls one block deeper inside the building using dark logs. Place glass panes at the centre for windows, with wooden planks above and below.

7

One block above the window (and one block further out) place normal logs.

8

The two side walls have a slightly different construction. At the highest level, place wooden plank blocks. These should be covered with dark wooden plank slabs attached to the roof.

9

At the rear of the house you can fill the wall as you want. Here, we used upside-down wooden plank stairs with wooden plank blocks at the lower level.

10

In front of the warehouse set two doors, placed from the inside of the building. Add stairs leading to the doors and torches that will shine in the dark.

11

Inside the warehouse you can build whatever you like: stairs, an anvil, an enchanting table, brewing stands and chests will all fit the theme. You could also build a ceiling and add lighting.

12

Build a few chimneys and add steampunk character by making white smoke from spiderweb blocks. To make the roof more complex you could add a small window.

Designed for a rollercoaster contest, the main element of *Spaghetti Rollercoaster* is a winding track that traverses the island world. However, Daniel also added a giant Ferris wheel and houses to bring more life to the build.

EMERALD HEART

THE GAME

Emerald Heart is a heroic-fantasy-themed MMORPG (massively multiplayer online roleplaying game) filled with epic stories and quests for the players to undertake. The palace and grounds contain hidden locations, statues and balconies, with plenty of secrets to find (including gold, which is hidden all around).

The build's creator, 'MrBatou,' was inspired initially by a picture featuring the rich emerald colour as part of a building. However, he quickly abandoned 'reality' and let his imagination lead the way instead. In many ways he is concerned that there is now too much detail in the buildings, and in other ways he feels there's not enough; overall, though, he is pleased with his creation and feels it has its charms.

THE BUILDER

MrBatou is from France, where he has been playing Minecraft® for many years. During this time he has built a number of breathtaking architectural creations – often featuring highly distinctive looks and styles – that have wowed the Minecraft community. The motif in *Emerald Heart* is the striking, emerald-coloured, domed palace rooftops that showcase his ability to bring a richness that is rarely seen in this type of building.

There is just as much going on beneath the stunning visuals of his impressive maps, with plenty of hidden secrets, discoverable paths and rooms, and collectables of all kinds. These not only enhance gameplay, but also guide the player through the architecture, encouraging them to explore every element in an interactive way.

Type of game: MMORPG
Difficulty: Easy
Time to play: Months
Number of players: Unlimited

Shaders and mods used: KUDA Shaders
Time to build: 100 hours

**PARKOUR AND
ROLLERCOASTERS**

DOME AND BRIDGE

The key to *Emerald Heart* is the green domes and the bridges – if you can create these, the rest will fall into place more easily. So let's look at how to build a dome and a bridge!

1

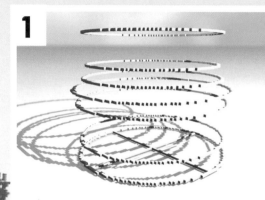

This building is round, so start by creating rings to suggest the sides of the building. Make some a little wider to vary the shape.

2

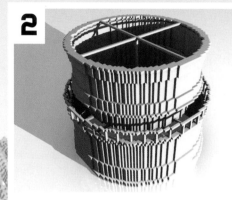

Fill between the rings to create walls.

3

A plugin such as WorldEdit can help you make your domed roof more easily. Add pillars to the walls and roof to add detail.

4

Add windows and further details. If you have any blank areas increase the level of detail. If you create and repeat small shapes these will help to unify the build.

5

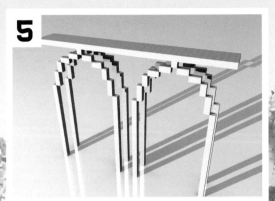

With the domed roof complete, let's tackle a small bridge. Start by tracing the path on top and the curved supports below.

6

Fill the walls and create a smaller passageway to act as a viaduct.

7

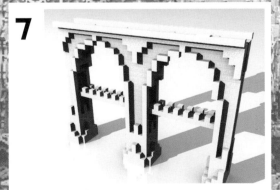

Build out from the basic shape to give it a more solid and detailed appearance.

8

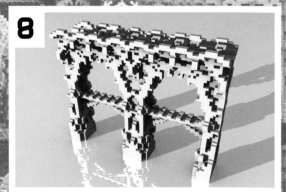

Add detail to every part of the structure using vaults, guardrails and buttresses.

Once you've mastered bridges and domes you can start to combine them to make your own city!

ECHOES FROM THE DEEP

THE GAME

Everbloom Studios' map, *Echoes from the Deep*, is set underwater, with a rich coral reef and a castle that resembles the type seen in a lot of domestic fish tanks. To fit the lore behind the map, the team decided to create three distinct areas for the map: a cyberpunk area, a 'biopunk' area and the main castle.

The parkour in the map is hard at times, but the team says it's not the most difficult game out there. In total, it takes about three hours to explore the map fully and finish all the parkour, which includes collecting all the diamonds at the end. Perhaps the most fun part of the map is the biggest challenge – parkouring the main castle, all the way to the top. It takes patience to get there (and a certain amount of trial and error), but the experience is definitely worth it.

The team started by making parts of the main castle, as well as the more standard fish and coral. However, the builders quickly realised that the theme was slightly boring and too basic for their exacting standards. It was at this point that the team decided to spice things up by adding two new styles.

Combining three different styles was definitely something the builders struggled with during their creation, and they admit that they made mistakes along the way. However, the team is glad it stumbled across various problems, as it enabled the builders to adapt and improve in a short space of time: as a direct result of building *Echoes from the Deep*, the team's new maps have stronger, more coherent themes.

THE BUILDER

Tom has been playing Minecraft® since 2011. He initially spent around a year playing single player maps, before he got into the creative side of Minecraft, which resulted in him co-founding Everbloom Studios. Like many builders, Tom particularly enjoys tackling things that no one has done before. He loves it when his builds surprise people, and believes that his impressionistic work has been his most influential, showing the community what lighting can be like in Minecraft.

Type of game: Parkour
Difficulty: Hard
Time to play: 3 hours

Number of players: 1
Time to build: 400 hours over 3 weeks

**PARKOUR AND
ROLLERCOASTERS**

ORGANICS

This tutorial is a simple introduction to organics, which is a very difficult build area for newcomers. Here, we're going to go through the process of making a colourful tropical fish in the style of a Queen Angel Fish.

1

Start with a 'line of action'. This is the centre of mass along your fish, which you will build around in the following steps.

2

Build the rough silhouette of your fish and add simple details, such as fins and a tail.

3

Now that you have a basic outline you can start blocking out parts of the fish. Start with the mouth area and move backwards to the tail.

4

Finish the head and the fins in a different colour so you can tell these sections apart.

5

Flesh out the midsection of the fish, making sure to add some bright highlights to the fins at the top and bottom.

6

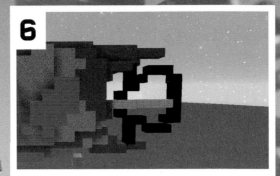

Start building out the tail section of the fish. Keep the shape fluid and flowing.

7

For the tail, start with some muted greens and slowly add more vibrant colours as you work backwards.

8

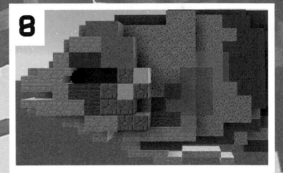

Work on the head and side-fins and add an eye using a Dragon Egg. This is probably the most difficult section to colour.

9

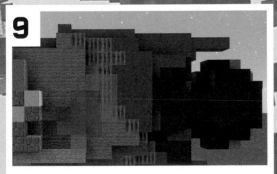

Colour the mid-section with some pastel yellows, oranges and greens. Fade the colour to green as you enter the tail section.

10

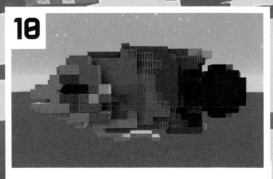

As you reach the back of the fish, make sure the tips of the tail are bright and vibrant compared to the main body.

TOM'S TIPS

TIP 1
When building, always keep the theme of your map in mind. If you want to implement other styles, try to make them fit with your overall theme.

TIP 2
With a big building it is useful to construct it completely from full blocks to start with. Then, give it more definition using detail blocks such as stairs and slabs.

TIP 3
If you're making organics for your build, try to give them an interesting pose, so it looks as if they are moving. This will make your map more dynamic.

119

ROLLERQUESTER

THE GAME

Rollerquester is an experimental rollercoaster adventure fused with a postmedieval theme. The adventure is based on redstone mechanisms and features lots of ways to interact with the rollercoaster, such as collecting items from chests and using a bow to shoot skeletons, all of which help you progress through the story.

The *Rollerquester* adventure is fairly easy when it's played in creative mode, but if you play in Survival mode there's a risk of death. In each case it's a short adventure that takes around 20 minutes to complete; Hans's big tip for making it the most fun is to cruise around the city when it's raining, with some fireworks going off and some great music playing.

As he was working to a time limit of three weeks (he was entering the finished adventure in an online competition), Hans quickly brushed up on redstone techniques and NBT (Named Binary Tag) commands and tried to wire his track to as many different interactions as possible.

Hans felt hugely satisfied with the final adventure and was particularly proud that he'd created something so complex around the simple theme of a rollercoaster ride. Given more time he would have liked to expand the game element, adding more minigames and a stronger storyline, but *Rollerquester* still taught Hans a lot about using redstone techniques and adventure-game making. It has subsequently formed the foundation for his own fictional multiverse – *The Arkade Kingdom*.

THE BUILDER

Hans (known as 'Destiny Gene' in Minecraft®) is an engineering student from the Philippines. He started playing Minecraft on a relative's computer and ended up binge-watching Minecraft videos on YouTube, in particular those on the incredibly popular 'Yogscast' channel. While the survival and city building elements of the game were fascinating enough, it was when he discovered adventure-map building and customisation that he realised the game's true potential.

Type of game: Adventure
(with minigames)
Difficulty: Medium
Time to play: 20 minutes
Number of players: 1

Minecraft version: Up to 1.7
Shaders and mods used: Minecraft Forge
ModLoader, Sonic Ether's Unbelievable
Shaders V10.1 Ultra, NBTedit, MCEdit
Time to build: 70 hours

ITEM SORTER

This item sorter uses hoppers and comparators to sort items into chests. The device can be used for adventures involving item delivery and for 'harvesting' quests. It can also be used for bank storage and checkpoints, where the player can deposit items in an adventure. In *Rollerquester* it is used for a fishing sidequest.

1

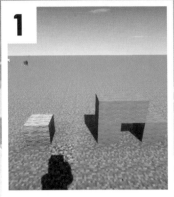

Place down green and blue wool as shown. Blue stands for sorted items and green is the sorting process.

2

Put down four hoppers. The two at the bottom face dirt in one direction; the third faces dirt in another direction; and the top one is 'clear'.

3

Remove the dirt and place a chest in front of the bottom hopper.

4

Put a redstone torch underneath the bottom hopper and redstone wire on the green wool.

5

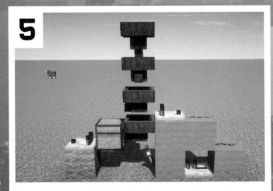

Put two comparators facing away from the bottom hopper and the chest. Put a repeater under the green wool, pointing towards the redstone torch.

6

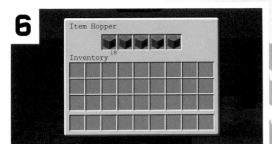

Fill the second hopper from the bottom with the item you want to sort out. Fill all the free spaces of the hopper.

7

One hopper isn't enough to sort every stacked item, so repeat steps 1–6 at the side of the original to ensure stacks of items are sorted out completely.

8

To sort more than one item, copy steps 1–7. Fill the hoppers of each device with new items. The last hopper in the line should be facing down.

9

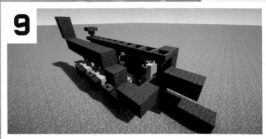

For returning unsorted items, a minecart track can be connected. Remove the dirt block under the last hopper and place red wool as shown.

10

Add a comparator facing away from the last hopper. Wire the comparator with redstone and a torch.

11

Lay track on the red wool, and place a redstone torch underneath the ramp. Put a button at the end.

12

Replace the ends of the track with red wool. Put a chest cart beside the button for unsorted items.

PARKOUR AND ROLLERCOASTERS: ROLLERQUESTER

HANS'S TIPS

TIP 1

You can base an adventure around the special effects
and redstone you want to incorporate, such as story
and dialogue, fireworks or intense boss battles. Make
several copies of one mechanism that you plan to
use repeatedly, but evolve it as you go so it becomes
progressively more challenging.

TIP 2

When activating circuits through multiple switches,
try using redstone logic gates like AND or OR so
they combine two inputs, such as switches, levers and
pressure plates. For example, you might design a circuit
so three people have to stand on three pressure plates
simultaneously to open a secret door.

TIP 3

Use comparators to send a redstone signal when they
detect an item in a container or a change in state. You
could use this to create a quest about delivering items
to a chest or a hopper, for example.

CHAPTER 3 SURVIVAL

LA BROCANTERIE

THE GAME

La Brocanterie is a survival game set in a vast, colourful, surreal world. It is a circular map, composed of five biomes with varied relief, eccentric architecture and creatures, as well as a large network of underground passages and other secret places. Every location is accessible by paths and stairs, which makes travel easy and fluid.

THE BUILDER

'Schnogot' is a student from Quebec, Canada, with an interest in music, philosophy and spirituality. Although he doesn't consider himself a 'gamer', Minecraft® caught his interest immediately. His first forays into building were mansions and castles, before he moved on to superstructures and giant fantasy constructions.

While Schnogot receives invitations to work with other people (and will collaborate occasionally), the dramas that sometimes flare up between community members mean that he generally prefers to build on his own. At the moment, with less free time available, Schnogot is working on smaller fantasy projects inspired by music and books.

Type of game: Survival
Difficulty: Varied
Time to play: Up to 1 hour
Number of players: 48

Shaders and mods used: GLSL shaders
mod with RudoPlays shaders
Time to build: 200 hours

SURVIVAL

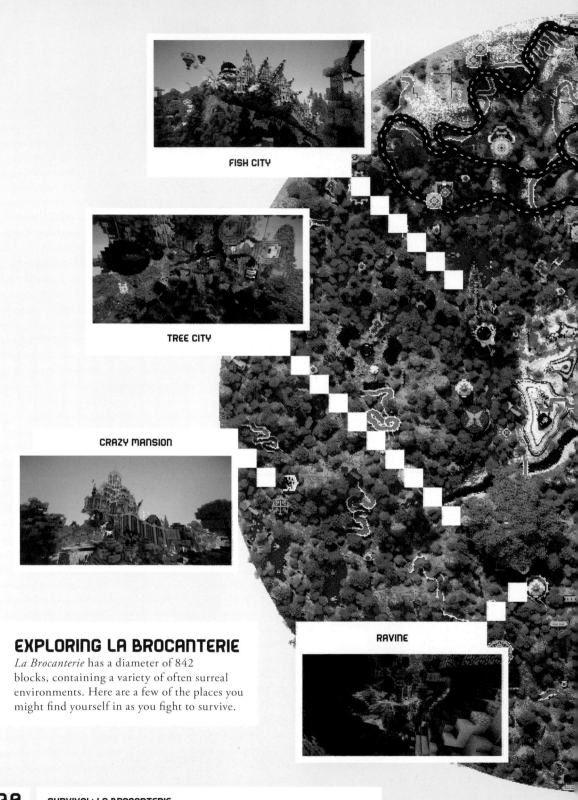

FISH CITY

TREE CITY

CRAZY MANSION

RAVINE

EXPLORING LA BROCANTERIE

La Brocanterie has a diameter of 842 blocks, containing a variety of often surreal environments. Here are a few of the places you might find yourself in as you fight to survive.

MOUNTAIN AND BIKE ROAD VILLAGE

SWAMP HOUSES

PONY LABYRINTH

ORGANIC LABYRINTH

A maze can be a great distraction for the players in a game (as it is in *La Brocanterie*), or it can form the main part of an adventure (as is the case with many 'dungeon crawlers'). In this tutorial we're going to look at how you can build an organic labyrinth above ground.

1

Build the outline of your labyrinth with the block of your choice. Determine the general trajectory of the pathway leading from the entrance to the exit using a bright and contrasting colour block; this will create a guide.

2

Use your labyrinth block to build the corridor for the correct path. Make sure that the corridor is wide enough for the player to move comfortably through it.

3

Remove most of the guide blocks you set out in step 1, retaining just a few as a reminder of the 'correct' path. Then, open some spaces in the corridor to build a network of dead ends.

4

Raise the height of the walls. You need to make sure that the players will not be able to escape by jumping over the walls, especially if your labyrinth is not built on flat terrain.

5

Add some colour and height variation to your walls to make them pleasing to the eye.

6

Bring your labyrinth to life by adding plants, flowers and any other decoration you can think of. Build an attractive entrance and exit to your labyrinth. You can do this by making an arch from a new material.

7

Add some trees to the top of the thicker wall sections. This will help to make the maze more confusing from above.

8

Place a discreet – yet distinctive – sign along the correct path of your labyrinth (such as ferns or mushrooms) to help you remember it!

9

Once you can find your way in (thanks to your personal sign), remove the remainder of the contrasting guide blocks you added in step 1.

10

Finally, add hazardous elements such as cobwebs, dense vines or even lava! This will increase the difficulty for the player.

ERONEV 2: SOUL CAULDRON

THE GAME

Eronev 2: Soul Cauldron started life as a survival game: a harsh land with no greenery, lots of monsters and difficult puzzles. There are few rules, so players can – for the most part – do whatever they want, whenever they want, whether that's breaking blocks, building bridges, using water to harden lava, or anything else that's necessary to progress.

Eronev 2: Soul Cauldron is very difficult. You are isolated and alone in a foreign, hostile land and must keep your wits about you to survive. The game can be completed in less than one hour if you rush, but there are a lot of extra things to collect, which can extend the playing time to over six hours.

The game's builder, Jigarbov, wanted to include a variety of puzzles, but finding the right balance was difficult: if a game is too hard, the story can easily be overshadowed, as the player focuses too much on survival. However, if it's too easy, a game won't present enough of a challenge. To come up with the best balance, Jigarbov made and tested his puzzles before he imported them into the world using MCEdit, tweaking their design to fit the game.

When it was launched, *Eronev 2: Soul Cauldron* was a pioneer in genre-bending custom maps. However, it has never been as successful or as popular as Jigarbov feels it should have been. He feels that with the first written dialogue, randomised mob loot and open-ended map design it may simply have been too far ahead of its time.

Type of game: Adventure/Survival/
CTM crossover
Difficulty: Hard
Time to play: Variable
Number of players: 1–4

Shaders and mods used: MCEdit with
TexelElf's filters
Minecraft version: 1.9
Time to build: 300 hours

SURVIVAL

THE BUILDER

Eronev 2: Soul Cauldron was created by the experienced Minecraft® adventure mapmaker, Jigarbov. When the map was made, the mapmaking community as a whole was going through a highly creative period and certain genres of maps were becoming more clearly defined: CTM ('Complete The Monument') maps were popular; adventure maps were becoming more prominent; and puzzle maps were also starting to emerge.

However, while individual genres were evolving, there wasn't much deviation from those predefined styles and few people were making 'crossover' games. The idea of mixing genres was something that Jigarbov wanted to explore with *Eronev 2: Soul Cauldron*, which also marked the first time he sought help with his maps. A friend, 'TexelElf', helped by creating a set of custom filters, which are plugins used by MCEdit to perform actions in the world. In one section, for example, TexelElf's filters help make a building look as if it is disintegrating, with the particles floating upwards.

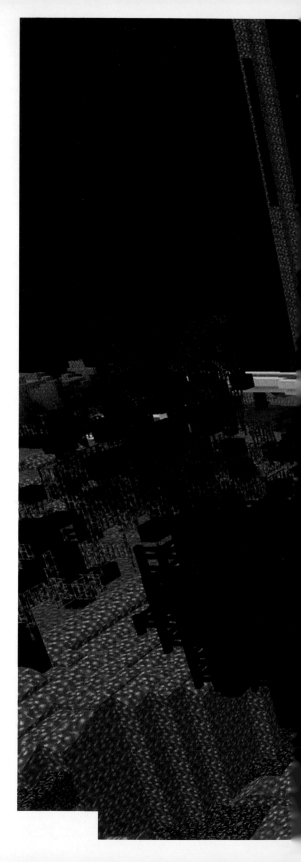

BARRIER BLOCKS

The barrier block is a block you can only get with a command – you won't find it in the creative inventory. Unlike regular blocks, barrier blocks don't have any texture that you can see, unless you're holding them in your hand. This means you can use them to create complex puzzles: you can give yourself one of these blocks with the command: /give @p barrier.

The red icons in the screenshot above are barrier blocks, which are invisible to the player. What the player will see is the puzzle below, which has water flowing haphazardly through the air!

LAVA AND FIREBALLS

You can use commands to control fire and lava in a range of ways, but often, it only takes a small change to make a big difference:

- With the command /summon FallingSand ~ ~10 ~ {Block:minecraft:flowing_lava",Time:1} you will summon a falling block of lava. When it hits the ground, it will spread.

- For something a little stranger, use this command: /summon FallingSand ~ ~10 ~ {Block:"minecraft:lava",Time:1} This will also summon a block of falling lava, but when it lands it will just sit there!

- How about some explosives? Try this: /summon Fireball ~ ~2 ~ {ExplosionPower:10,direction:[0.0,0.0,0.0]} When you use this command it will summon an explosive fireball that you can punch with your hand. Be careful, though, as the fireball can leave a huge crater in the direction you punch it!

- If you reduce the ExplosionPower value in the previous command, the fireball will cause less destruction.

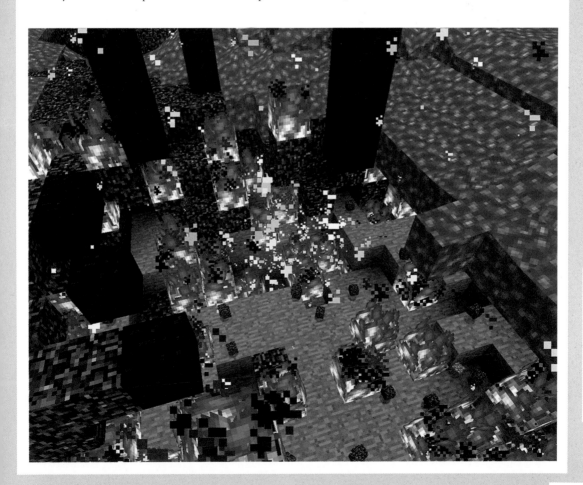

THE RISEN DEAD

THE GAME

The Risen Dead has a spooky amusement park theme that creates a scary clash of dark dread and bright, jolly colours. Sunfury had to re-create lots of the classic rides you would expect to find at a carnival, which serve as the backdrop for the waves of zombies you have to defeat.

A scoreboard keeps track of how well you do, making this kind of map ideal for multiplayer games, with teams of players pitted against one another, as well as solo play.

THE BUILDER

Sunfury is a large team of builders focused on creating games for the Minecraft® community. The team originated as a group of friends who just wanted to make minigames, but it has developed into a much larger and more ambitious organisation that also works on large, complex structures used for gaming events and by YouTubers to create videos.

Founded in 2013 by Janakin, Sunfury brought together a team of experienced builders who were able to start creating great work right away. *The Risen Dead* was the team's first game, inspired by the horde modes seen in shooters such as *Call of Duty*.

Many of the team members have considered careers in game development, and feel that making games within Minecraft has taught them a great deal. Part of their success comes from having builders with different areas of expertise and interest, with some members focusing on terrain, others on design and a few concentrating on 'wiring up' elements to make them interactive. Janakin points out that analysing human behaviour is also important, and that when making games you have to understand what people might do within the play areas and take that into account.

Type of game: Minigame
Difficulty: Selectable
Time to play: 15 minutes

Number of players: Multiplayer
Shaders and mods used: MCEdit
Time to build: 1 week

MAKING MINIGAMES

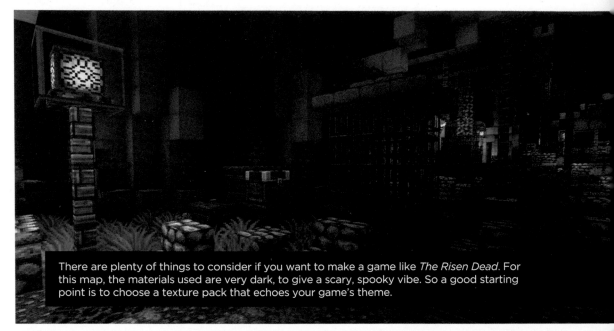

There are plenty of things to consider if you want to make a game like *The Risen Dead*. For this map, the materials used are very dark, to give a scary, spooky vibe. So a good starting point is to choose a texture pack that echoes your game's theme.

You need to think about the layout of your map. With a game of this type the map needs to flow, with no dead ends for the player to get stuck in.

Once you've created your various components, paste them into the map layout using a world-editing plugin. Add foliage, paths and benches to fill out the map and link the separate components.

If you're creating a multiplayer game you need to consider a few extra things. For example, you will need to use the code @a, instead of @p in command blocks that target a player. This will ensure that all players are targeted by the command block, rather than a single player.

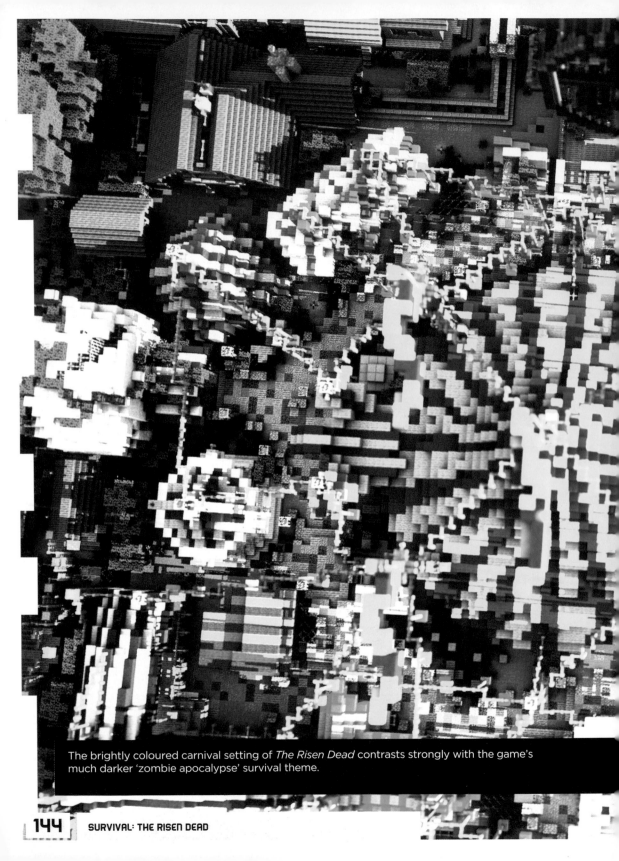

The brightly coloured carnival setting of *The Risen Dead* contrasts strongly with the game's much darker 'zombie apocalypse' survival theme.

INFINITY DUNGEON

THE GAME

Infinity Dungeon was designed as a random, ever-changing dungeon that you can replay as many times as you like and always find something new. The basic premise is that you have to find five crystals. As you search the dungeon you will discover various types of armour, weapons and tools that can both help and hinder you. The game takes its inspiration from dungeon crawlers, and every time you regenerate the map you are set back a significant amount.

Infinity Dungeon was one of the first Minecraft® maps of its kind to be released at this scale and it proved very popular. However, it's impossible to gauge *Infinity Dungeon's* difficulty, as it uses a randomly generated layout based on a number of different room templates. Within these rooms there are chests, monsters and obstacles that are also generated randomly. As a result, you could find yourself with an extremely difficult game that might last for hours, or a very easy quest that is over in 30 minutes. It is theoretically possible to have all five crystals appear right next to your starting point, so you could win in a matter of minutes (although that's highly unlikely!).

After sorting out the tech (which relied heavily on Minecraft 1.8's /clone command), the next step was designing a number of rooms that could be copied and pasted into the dungeon. The design of each room had a number of characteristics, including limited entrances and exits, chest locations and designs that would make each room distinct. Later, the builder, Jigarbov, included palette swaps, so the colour of leaves or some other blocks would change, giving even greater variety.

The final stage was testing the map and launching it, although before he released a final version of the game, Jigarbov made several balancing changes. The reception of the map was excellent, and its creator feels it is still one of the most fleshed-out randomly generated dungeons for Minecraft. The nature of the map may mean that some people don't get the experience he intended, but it has also meant that many people have had an even better one than he could have hoped for!

Type of game: Minigame
Difficulty: Random
Time to play: Variable
Number of players: 1–4

Shaders and mods used: MCEdit,
TexelElf's filters
Time to build: 100 hours

SURVIVAL

THE BUILDER

Jigarbov has made a lot of maps over the course of his Minecrafting career, and while this project was built in under three days, it has more play hours than any of his previous creations.

When Minecraft® 1.8 was released, the command /clone was the first of a swathe of exciting features. Inspired by the new command, Jigarbov halted development on everything else he was working on and focused on the idea of a fully realised, randomly generated dungeon. At the time of development it was possible to put a command block inside a dispenser and it would dispense a random command block. This was an extremely simple and fast method to produce the results that he wanted, and Jigarbov completed the first version of his dungeon in three days. However, the random command block feature was open to abuse, and in time it was removed.

Minecraft 1.8 also introduced things such as scoreboards, statistics and resource packs, which meant you could change any block to whatever you could create a model of. Use of the /clone command, being able to target entities with commands, and the ability to update the contents of tile entities with block data all brought Minecraft much closer to becoming the game development tool that many players already used it as. It also meant a lot more work needed to be done by the mapmakers in terms of coding, modelling and game design. Jigarbov soon realised that having more options meant his maps would be more complex and the development times for his adventures would be longer!

TRAPS

Traps are a hallmark of any good dungeon game, but they take skill to create. A well-designed trap should give the player an opportunity to discover it, so even if they fall into the trap they'll see their mistake, learn from the experience, and remember it in the future. With that in mind, let's make a trap.

1

Start by making a small area for the trap.

2

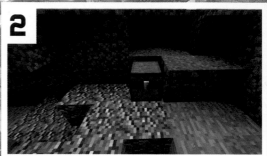

Mimics are monsters that can change shape and are often portrayed as a chest. Conveniently, Minecraft® comes with something called a 'trapped chest', which you can find in the creative menu.

3

Break the block that is two blocks beneath the trapped chest and put down a dot of redstone dust. When the player opens the chest it will power the redstone. Don't open the chest again until you finish the next couple of steps.

4

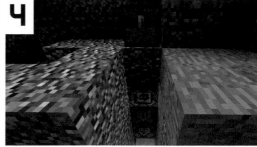

Under that dot of redstone add two command blocks. Make sure they are both pointing downwards (you can tell the direction they are pointing by the triangle on them). Give them both the command /give @p command_block.

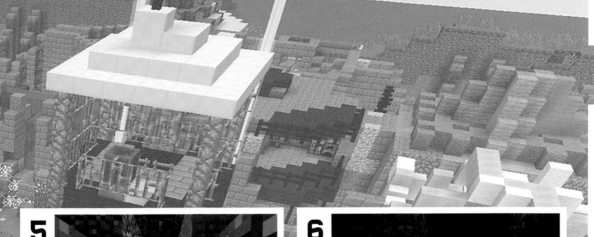

5

Right-click the bottom command block. Make sure it is set to 'Chain' and 'Always Active', as this will ensure that it runs at the same time as the upper, orange command block.

6

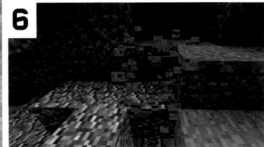

On the orange command block type /setblock ~ ~3 ~ minecraft:air 0 destroy. Now, when the chest is opened, it will be destroyed with a satisfying pop!

7

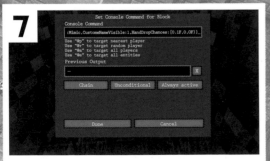

On the green command block enter the following command: /summon Skeleton ~ ~4 ~ {HandItems: [{Count:1,id:woodenaxe,tag:{display:{Name:Mimic Axe,Lore:[Not very strong...]}}},{}],ArmourItems: [{},{},{},{id:chest}],CustomName:Mimic,HandDrop Chances:[0.1F,0.0F]}.

8

Now, when the player tries to open the chest a Mimic appears! Because you are using a trapped chest, there is a slight red colouring on the latch. This gives the player a clue that something fishy is going on, but they won't know what it is...

CUBE BLOCK

THE GAME

The *Cube Block* world is a cube, which is, of course, made of Minecraft® cubes, so in this way it is a 'world within a world'. The player only has the resources of a small map, and needs to earn a number of achievements to make the playtime longer.

To create *Cube Block*, Simon started with a lava core. Then came a big stone layer containing caves, dungeons, lava/water lakes, mineshafts and other secrets for the players to find. On top of the stone is earth or sand, with the other sides of the world utilising a different biome and style: the top is a normal plains biome; the sides are desert, jungle, forest and ice taiga; and at the bottom is a small lake with a boat.

Simon is very proud of *Cube Block*. The game currently has more than 80,000 downloads, making it his most successful and well-known game to date. Simon is now working on a new tree pack and some mods.

THE BUILDER

Known as 'RexRaptor' in Minecraft, Simon Biebl is from Germany. Before he found Minecraft, Simon was a fan of the online game, *LEGO® Universe*, but when that game closed down its servers he began to search for an alternative. The links between LEGO and Minecraft are obvious, as they are both about using blocks to build things, and Simon quickly found kindred spirits in this new creative community.

Although he has worked with build teams in the past and run servers, Simon now prefers to work on his own, creating highly original designs. Simon's area of expertise is in building minigames and survival maps, but his interest in game design and programming reaches beyond Minecraft to the point that he'd like to make it his profession.

Type of game: Survival
Difficulty: Medium
Number of players: 1–10

Shaders and mods used: Edits Shader
Ultra, MCEdit, Map Making Tools mod
Time to build: Approx. 10 hours

VERTICAL WORLD

It took Simon around 10 hours to build *Cube Block*, with each side using a different biome. This walkthrough shows you how to build a simple terrain on one side of a cube-based map; from here you could go on to build a more elaborate landscape.

1

The first thing you need is a stone layer as a base for your terrain; you can add ores and other stone variants.

2

Build a dirt layer on top of the stone (for other biomes you can use sand or snow). For this side use podzol, because the texture is similar to dirt.

3

Next you'll need to create hills and valleys. With water you will need to use secret barrier blocks or a program such as MCEdit to prevent the water from flowing downwards.

4

Once you've finished terraforming, build some large structures, such as houses, bridges, or maybe some towers.

5

Add some smaller buildings to the map so the player has more places to explore. Here we've added a path to the house, chopped logs, a fireplace and a cave entrance.

6

Depending on your biome, use different logs for trees. Place a variety of flowers and plants under the trees.

7

Add leaves to your trees, building them in the shape shown here.

8

Delete random edges from the lower leaf sections, as well as leaves at the top, so the overall shape looks more like a cross.

9

Repeat the previous steps to add leaves to the rest of your trees. Once all of the trees are done, your map is finished!

Cube Block is slightly harder than a lot of survival maps, not least because there are lots of challenges to complete: not falling off is the hardest part!

THE PORT OF FRONTIER

THE GAME

The Port of Frontier is set during the Japanese Industrial Revolution and is based on historical records from that time (Japan's 'Meiji period'). Although it is primarily a story-mode map with talking non-player characters, the team behind it has designed the map in such a way that it is also the perfect backdrop for survival games.

However, even with a huge team, the project took eight months to complete. This was primarily because each region on the map is loaded with so much detail – as you walk around you can even interact with the ornaments and items within a house or factory! The project scale is also slightly 'larger than life' at 1:1.5, which has enabled the team to magnify some of the carvings on walls and in homes, further adding to the immersive authenticity of the build.

THE BUILDER

Founded in 2013, LinsCraft is a group of builders and creators from China, which now consists of more than 100 members, each working on individual projects for different purposes. The team started out designing architectural features (with a focus on Chinese architecture), but has expanded into mapmaking and fantasy worlds, including a huge candy tree for children and a fantasy artwork, *Magical Whale*.

For LinsCraft, Minecraft® is a design tool that can be adapted and used by anyone. One of its aims is to advocate the beauty of classical architecture and use its maps to inspire other talented designers and architects. In doing so it hopes to become the 'best of the best' design teams – not just in Minecraft, but in graphics and architectural design as well.

Type of game: Survival
Difficulty: Variable
Time to play: Hours
Time to build: Eight months

One of the most striking things about *The Port of Frontier* is the attention to detail. The team's research included carefully studying the construction materials used during the period and emulating them in Minecraft® to keep the build as authentic as possible.

貫彻叭爷童要思想,安全第一,狠抓生产!
怒肝三年! 勤洗脸来勤洗手,大建出奇迹!!

The LinsCraft team initially focused on creating architectural features, but now has a much broader repertoire that includes maps like *The Port of Frontier*, which took eight months to bring to fruition.

THE CRYPTE OF THE DEATH

THE GAME

The Crypte of the Death is a massively multiplayer online roleplaying game (MMORPG) with a dark and creepy map. The environment is cavernous and lonesome, which makes it quite scary, but also strangely appealing to explore. As the cave is such a vast, dark playing space, small details can be difficult to pick out, and you can easily become lost – perhaps stuck for many hours. If this wasn't the case, and you didn't die, the dungeon could be completed pretty quickly, but the darkness and difficulty mean that you *will* die in this game!

THE BUILDER

MrBatou is a Minecraft® architect from France. Although his building work is often architectural, it also includes many organic forms, some hyperrealistic work and many builds that defy categorisation: he is always looking to create the impossible or improbable.

MrBatou is also a big fan of games such as *Dark Souls*, where challenge-hungry players thrive on difficult games that require plenty of patience to complete the quest. This is very much how he treats all of his projects in Minecraft, and in this game he brings the challenge to you, the player.

Type of game: MMORPG
Difficulty: Hard
Time to play: Months

Number of players: Unlimited
Time to build: 200 hours

SURVIVAL

GOTHIC TOWER

The dark, gothic feel of *The Crypte of the Death* is echoed by its architecture, which includes beautifully crafted domed towers that creep out from the shadows. Here's how they can be made:

1

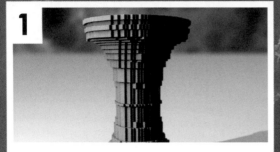

Trace the outline of a large circular tower to form the basic shape of your tower and then fill inside to create the walls, editing your curve if it is not quite right.

2

Next is the challenging part: you need to decorate your base. You don't need too much detail, but adding pikes and arabesques will give you a suitably textured finish.

3

Create a tower stand using pillars and then add the platform they support. Space out your pillars evenly.

4

Expand the bottom and top of the pillars to make them look more solid. If the middle of the columns looks a little empty you could also add detail there.

5

Add a second platform above the first. Make its supporting columns longer or shorter than those of the first platform to add variety.

6

In this build the pillars are very small, so they don't need much detail adding to them.

7

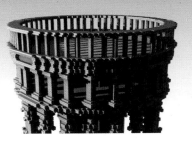

It's a good idea to build in threes, as it prevents builds appearing too symmetrical. Add a third row of thinner columns. As you won't see them clearly on a big building like this, these columns don't have to be perfectly even.

8

This tower has a dome – there are plugins that can help you make a perfect sphere. Place a small circle on top of the dome to be used for the 'nest'.

9

To make the dome more ornate, place some raised curves along the roof, leading to some pillars and a small platform on top. As this platform is small, you can use undetailed pillars.

10

Make another, smaller domed roof. Add more raised curves to the smaller dome and make an ornate spire to mark the top – this is the ideal spot for a flag!

The Crypte of the Death is an intentionally dark environment that is designed to instil a sense of dread in the player: who knows what's lurking in the shadows or around the next unlit corner!

CHAPTER 4 BATTLES

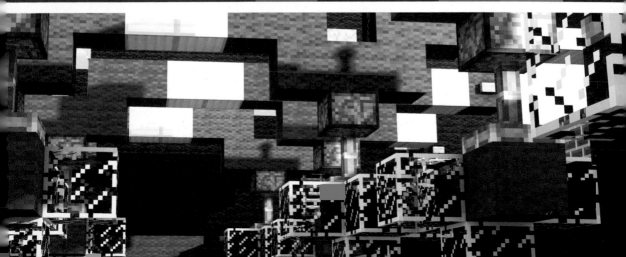

NAVORATH VALLEY

THE GAME

Navorath Valley is a unique player vs. player (PvP) map created by the members of goCreative. The map is based on multiple biomes that include Western, Redwood Forest and Alpine. Each biome has a different climate and architectural style, with each building housing an intricately designed interior to enhance the in-game experience.

You spawn in a giant castle and then descend into the valley to fight for your life. With a wide variety of custom objects, winding roads, paths and many hidden treasures and details within the virtual environment, *Navorath Valley* is an exciting PvP map that will allow you to play for hours with your friends. There are exploding trains, dangerous pirate air balloons, ships and more to keep you on your toes!

THE BUILDER

Brandon Relph is the CEO and co-founder of the goCreative team. Running the team alongside his German counterpart, Florian Funke, Brandon has moved from developing their creative server to the business and community side of being in the Minecraft® world. Consequently, he now spends a lot of his time taking care of their big clients, PR and business events.

Minecraft caught Brandon's attention because of the great community surrounding it and its highly unique style. He believes that the key to every game lies in the planning and that it's important to really pay attention at the start of every build. *Navorath Valley* was made for a public server known as MineVast, which is really happy with how the game turned out, as is goCreative.

Type of game: PvP
Difficulty: Medium
Time to play: 1 hour+

Number of players: Unlimited
Time to build: 200 hours

BATTLES

BRANDON'S TIPS

TIP 1
The interior of a build is as important as its exterior. However, you need to make sure it is built to the same scale using different types of blocks and elements.

TIP 2
Look at images of real buildings and use these as a reference for your builds.

TIP 3
Always build on the scale the map is made for. If you are building a PvP map make sure everything is relative to the size of a player.

MEDIEVAL TABLE

One of the great things about *Navorath Valley* is the detailing to the interior of the buildings, as well as their exterior, so don't forget to add detail to both! In this tutorial we look at how you can build a medieval-style table of a type that appears within the game.

1

To build this table you will need a 15x11 block area. Make sure you have enough space and add a layout frame using placeholder/layout blocks of your choice.

2

Create a 3x3 table foot by placing dark oak wood planks. Surround this block with dark oak wood stairs facing towards the centre. Add a 3x3 area on top of it using dark oak wood planks.

3

Build another three table feet at the remaining corners of your layout frame, and then remove the frame (it was only a guide to make sure you had enough space).

4

Add three upside-down dark oak wood stairs to the four table feet. These should face inwards, towards the opposite pair of feet.

5

Cover the remaining empty space between the tops of the table feet with dark oak wood slabs.

6

Once you have the tabletop in place, find its centre and add a 3x3 area of grass blocks.

7

Place upside-down jungle wood stairs around the grass created in step 6 and add jungle wood slabs at the corners.

8

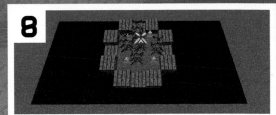

Add a flower design to the grass, using tall flowers in a cross shape at the centre and smaller flowers at the corners. You can pick your own flowers or use the design shown here.

9

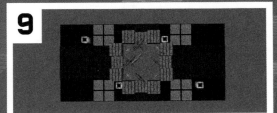

Now it's time to add decorations to the table, such as place settings made from stone pressure plates, a tablecloth made using carpet, or even coffee pots made by adding player heads.

10

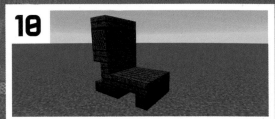

Your table needs chairs, so use spruce wood stairs to create a laying down 'L' shape. On top of that add two note blocks, and finish it off with two spruce wood stairs on top.

11

Add two trapdoors to each side of your chair to act as armrests and then use carpet to create a seat.

12

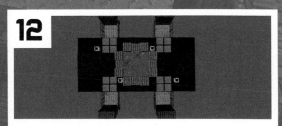

You can add as many chairs as you want to the table to complete your design.

Navorath Valley is built around a variety of biomes, each with its own distinct style. These biomes include Alpine (top left), Redwood Forest (bottom left and top right) and Western (bottom right).

PHAIN

THE GAME

Phain is a vast map covering a land area in excess of 13½ million blocks, with an extra 9½ million blocks with air! It's hardly surprising that it took its builder around 400 hours to make, and is his most complex build to date.

The map was inspired by a video game called *Endless Legend* and is based on a large mass of land known as *Phain*. Although the people and creatures that resided there were peaceful and nomadic, a race of nefarious giants plagued the land. Over time these giants carved lakes and dragged mountains until they had transformed *Phain* into a land that resembled a hex-based game board. You are a new settler on this land – what you will do with it is up to you!

According to its builder, Andrzej Czerniewski (better known as 'Darastlix'), *Phain* can be used in many different ways. You can play regular single-player survival on it, or it can be played on a large server with friends. You could use *Phain* on an RPG server, for example, and create kingdoms, conquer new hexes and trade with other players, or you could use it as a 'creative plots' server, where each player gets his or her own hex to build on.

At first, Darastlix thought that making this map would prove impossible: nobody had ever made hexagonal terrains in the past and there were no tools available to make them. However, rather than give up, Darastlix coded his own custom generator in Python, then used World Machine to build a complex network consisting of 421 nodes. At this point the map contained a total of 923 hexagons that he painstakingly filled by hand using a variety of premade custom objects in WorldPainter.

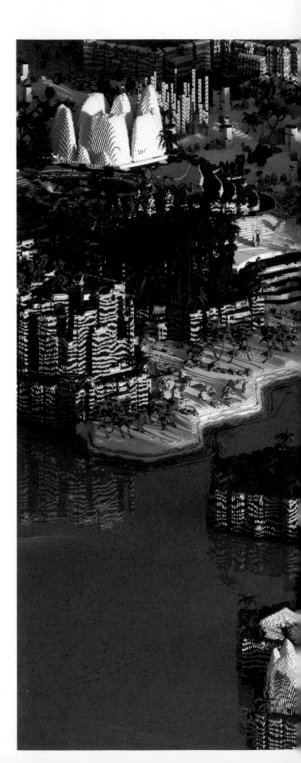

Type of game: Survival
Difficulty: Medium
Time to play: Days
Number of players: The more the better!
Minecraft version: 1.8 or above

Shaders and mods used: Python programming language, World Machine, WorldPainter, MCEdit, WorldEdit, VoxelSniper, and many other tools!
Time to build: 400 hours

THE BUILDER

Phain is the brainchild of Lithuanian builder, Darastlix, who is living in Poland while he works towards a Master's degree in Computer Science.

Darastlix got into Minecraft® when he was still at school. He played with friends on a private server where they built bases, destroyed them, fought each other, waged wars and tried to roleplay some kind of politics. At university he also started making maps and when a friend introduced him to the *Fall of an Empire* RPG server he decided to make a completely new map for them. The first map that he wasn't ashamed to show is called *Alerak*, which you can still download and play.

Today, Darastlix works for the BlockWorks build team, which has worked with Microsoft and Disney, as well as many other large companies, server networks and major YouTubers. As a specialist builder, Darastlix is best known for his very large, realistic, mythical terrains that have fantasy elements. His maps typically revolve around one simple theme, such as winter, gardens, balance, autumn, hexagons or whatever else comes to mind – the themes are usually random and don't have any pattern. At the moment, these maps are some of the most popular WorldPainter maps on the Internet.

DARASTLIX'S TIPS

TIP 1

Be ambitious, but also realistic. Many projects fail because they are too big or simply impossible.

TIP 2

Get inspired! It's OK to be inspired by other people: take their ideas and change them into yours. For this map, Darastlix was inspired by the *Endless Legend* video game.

TIP 3

Don't be afraid to experiment. When it was launched, nobody had seen anything like *Phain* in Minecraft.

WORLDPAINTER

Like many builders, Darastlix uses WorldPainter to create terrain. However, this is a rather complex programme, which requires plenty of practice before you can make the most of it.

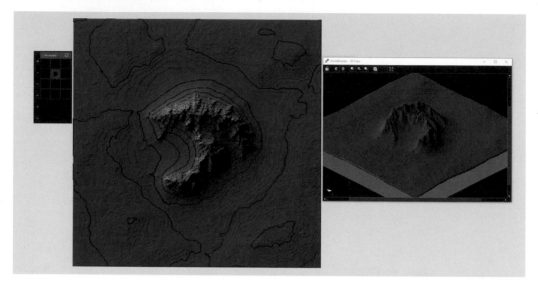

Using WorldPainter's Spray Paint tool you can selectively raise and lower the height of your 'world' to raise mountains and carve valleys into the landscape. Different brushes enable you to alter the topography with increasingly precise or broad strokes, depending on the brush's characteristics.

WORLDPAINTER TIPS

• You can download and install WorldPainter from www.worldpainter.net. However, you also need to ensure you have Java 8 installed.

• Thanks to the builder community there is a wide range of trees, brushes and other WorldPainter assets available, which means you don't always have to start from scratch. For *Phain*, Darastlix used premade custom trees created by Monsterfish and brushes by 'Lentebriesje' to speed up the process. These assets came from www.planetminecraft.com.

• If you're using premade items and tools it's a good idea to put everything into a single folder on your hard drive so you can find it easily.

WorldPainter's editing options allow you to determine the fundamental geography of your creation by changing the materials used to describe certain features (stone for mountains, for example). You can also add detail to your world by 'painting in' bushes (shown here in red) and trees (shown in yellow). In all instances your terrain and features can be refined, removed and edited as you go.

A finished WorldPainter terrain, exported into Minecraft®.

One of the most impressive elements of *Phain* is its scale: the land (and sea) covers an area of more than 13½ million blocks!

FOOSBALL TABLE

THE GAME

Foosball (or fuzboll, table football or table soccer, as it is also known) was invented in England in the early 1900s. The tabletop game has since enjoyed an enduring popularity that has seen it appear in bars and clubs around the globe, spawning leagues and even a World Cup competition in the process.

This playable Minecraft® foosball table comes from YouTube superstar 'SethBling'. Unlike its real-life counterpart, the game features three rows of foosball players per side that 'kick' the ball by pushing out water (which quickly recedes). An automatic score counter uses a sand display to keep track of who's winning, and the game is fully resettable.

In real life, foosball is pretty frustrating, and it's just the same with SethBling's Minecraft version. However, due to its similarity to its real-life counterpart, as well as its simplicity, this version of the game has proved highly popular: it's been downloaded tens of thousands of times, and had a million views on SethBling's YouTube channel.

THE BUILDER

Known as the 'King of Redstone', SethBling started his YouTube channel in 2006, making it one of the oldest on the site (which launched in early 2005). However, he didn't post his first video until 2011. Since then, his 'let's play' and building videos have received half a billion views and his channel has attracted more than two million subscribers.

SethBling is best known for his Minecraft minigames and contraptions, and for re-creating real-world games such as this foosball table. As well as being a big success in the Minecraft community, he is also known as a 'speed runner', and has held a number of records for the fastest play through particular games.

Type of game: Minigame
Difficulty: Easy
Time to play: Minutes

MCBCON ARENA

THE GAME

The *MCBCon Arena* is a 400x400 block 'build battle' arena, where creative minds join the server to duel it out and see who's the best builder. The arena contains four build areas on which the players build for an allotted time to a certain theme: once the time is up, the builds are judged and a winner is crowned!

Although it is up to the contenders to decide what fills the arena, a lot of time and thought went into the vistas they can see while they're there. The arena is inspired by the work of the artist Demizu Posuka, and offers a colourful mix of themes that are representative of the many build styles that will fill it during the battles. There are nods to all kinds of architecture, including fantasy, steampunk, medieval and modern, which are designed to make you feel as if you are the star of a match in a fantastical city.

The first area to be built was the main lobby in which the players arrive, after which the Everbloom Studios team focused on the basic shape of the arena. Once the arena's shape and size had been finalised, the team gradually added the structures that surround it, creating the arena's unique atmosphere.

THE BUILDER

Matt is the CEO of Everbloom Studios. He got into Minecraft® in 2012, so has a long-standing love for the game, which is fuelled by his creativity. In the early days he would spend hours mining just cobblestone and wood to build castles and mansions before the creepers could get them.

During the Minecraft Beta, Matt would take breaks from long-standing team projects and hop on random servers to see how fast he could get the maximum builder's rank. This was not only a great way for him to hone his building skills, but he also met a lot of talented people who he kept in contact with. A few years later he was invited to join a team called Mystic Absents, which eventually grew into Everbloom Studios. Today, Matt builds structures of all types, whether it's fantasy, steampunk, medieval, Victorian or baroque; the Everbloom team has experts in organics, terrain and other specialist areas.

Type of game: Arena
Difficulty: Easy

Time to play: Depends on the players!
Number of players: 4
Time to build: 100–120 hours

BATTLES

MATT'S TIPS

TIP 1

When building, always consider where the player will be standing. If you fly around a lot while making the map, you will see the build differently to how a player will see it. To craft the experience properly you need to see the build from the point of view of someone playing your map.

TIP 2

Always use reference pictures for your builds. Although your ideas may be great in your mind, the proportions may look off and buildings unsupported when you actually come to build them. If you have some pictures you can see how similar structures are made in the real world, which will make your buildings more believable and grounded.

SMALL-SCALE CITYSCAPES

You can turn any large, plain area into a small and colourful cityscape, adding atmosphere and scale to part of a build that might otherwise be uninteresting. If you have large buildings in the foreground, adding these small cityscapes in the distance – as is the case with *MCBCon Arena* – will enhance the feeling of scale through 'forced perspective'.

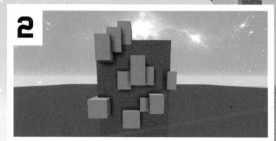

Start with a simple shape such as a cube or a rectangle that you would like to add a cityscape to. Make sure the object is relatively large so you have room to build on it.

Start adding shapes to the main face of the object and around the corners as shown. Make sure to vary their size and shape, as well as their position.

Add shapes to the top of the object, making sure that more distant objects are taller than those at the front. Make some floating and slanted shapes to draw the viewer's attention.

Begin to carve spaces for windows. Smaller windows will cause shapes to look larger, while larger windows make the shapes look smaller.

5

Fill the spaces behind the windows with sea lanterns for a 'glass' effect. Place fences over the sea lanterns. This will increase the feeling of scale.

6

Add some stone supports for the larger overhangs and any 'floating' buildings.

7

Place small wooden details made of wooden slabs and stairs to the unsupported buildings on the face. This will finish the walls and supports and you can add roofs.

8

The first type of roof for the buildings uses flat, round shapes; the second type uses diagonal roofs facing the viewer. These will make up the majority of the roofs in the cityscape, although you should leave the highest towers for now.

9

The third roof type is a conical design, which is best for the tall spires at the top of the cityscape. There are lots of different types, so experiment!

10

Finally, build up and chisel away at the original shape you have been building on to make it look more organic. Your miniature cityscape is now complete!

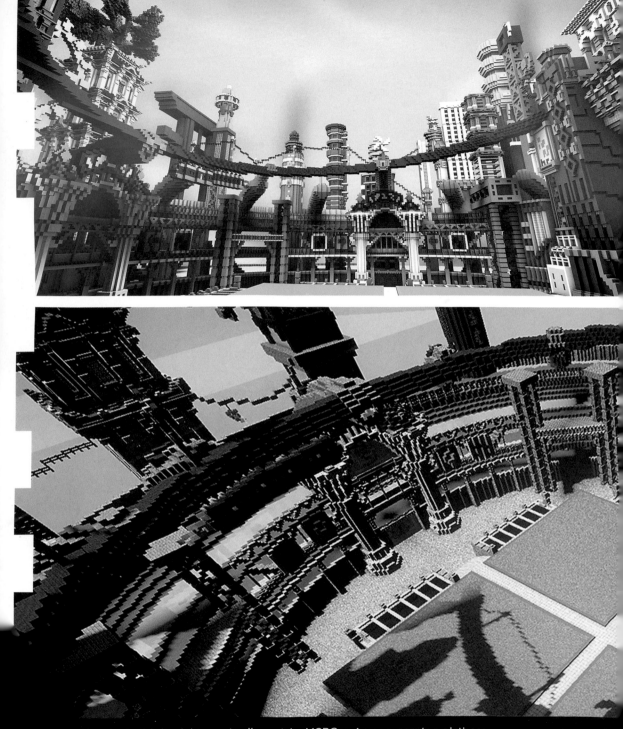

...ust like the builds it might eventually contain, *MCBCon Arena* presents a plethora ...different architectural styles.

CHAPTER 5 PUZZLE SOLVING

THE TOURIST

THE GAME

The Tourist takes place in the Montmartre district of Paris, where you can find the Sacré-Cœur Basilica. You play the tourist in the game's title, who wakes up on a sightseeing tour bus after taking a nap and realises that the city is devoid of life. As the game is played in Minecraft®'s peaceful mode you won't be fighting armies of creepers. Instead, the story follows your investigation into what has happened, as you face a number of puzzles and parkour elements along the way.

The Tourist wasn't originally created as a game. Having watched endless videos of players making things in Minecraft's creative mode, the game's builder, Loic Serra (aka 'Stratocrafter'), decided he wanted to make a large monument, and felt that the Sacré-Cœur would be a good challenge. Drawing on plans, photos and research, he spent hundreds of hours building the church, but it wasn't until he had completed his build that he learned it would be possible to use it as the starting point for his own adventure.

It takes around four hours to complete the story, particularly if you take the time to explore the world it is set in. This is well worth doing, as Loic has created a very beautiful setting with a lot of detail. Although he has a great interest in history (and was also inspired by a number of movies), most of the map was built to fit Loic's vision for his adventure, and it provides you with a relaxing and enjoyable playthrough.

Incredibly, *The Tourist* is the only thing that Loic has ever built in Minecraft. He is hugely proud of it and pleased with the public's response to it, but while players often ask him if he'll create a follow up, he doesn't think he'll ever make another Minecraft adventure.

Type of game: Adventure
Difficulty: Medium
Time to play: 4 hours

Number of players: 1
Shaders and mods used: Jolicraft
Time to build: 250 hours

THE BUILDER

Loic is a professional musician from Propriano in Corsica. When he's not playing music, Loic's playing video games; his favourite genres are roleplaying, sandbox and strategy. Loic found Minecraft® when he was looking for a browser game to quickly fill some free time, and started watching tutorials and learning how to do various things with the game.

When he revealed *The Tourist*, the Minecraft community accepted Loic with open arms. Not only did he receive praise from players around the world, but some community members translated the game's story into different languages, while others offered to help him develop various parts of the map. Yet despite the huge and supportive community, Loic primarily worked alone, as he felt his availability didn't really allow him to be part of a team. However, one particular supporter of his work – 'Occosop' – offered to improve the organ that is in the church in the game, and the results really impressed Loic.

LOIC'S TIPS

TIP 1

When re-creating a large, real-world monument, try to find plans of it or at least its dimensions. Use the grid tool in software such as Photoshop or Paint to convert it into 1x1m squares, the size of Minecraft blocks. You can then reproduce the floor using a flat map and use photographs from different angles to build it in a realistic way.

TIP 2

When building, try to make everything with odd number lengths. This helps make things symmetrical, as the centre of each part of the build will be located on one line of blocks (this is very useful for centring doors and windows).

TIP 3

Buttons may seem more modern than levers, but once you release them there is no more redstone signal. Using redstone latches solves this problem and will make the redstone signal active after you release the button. There are hundreds of these used in *The Tourist*.

CODED DOOR

When you build an adventure map you will often want the player to solve a puzzle before they can continue. As *The Tourist* demonstrates, the best way to do this is with a locked door. This tutorial will show you how to build a simple coded door that opens when you activate levers to enter the correct combination.

1

Start by building a frame for the door and the levers. Here we have a five-block space left for the levers, but you can add as many as you want – the more levers you have, the more combination options there are.

2

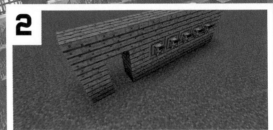

Place blocks in each space and place a lever on each. You must keep one block between the door and the levers.

3

Place a redstone torch at the rear side of the block where you put the levers and place two blocks under each torch.

4

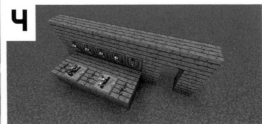

Place a redstone in front of the levers you want in your combination and a repeater in front of the others. Make sure the repeater is placed in the right direction.

5

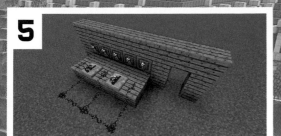

Link the redstone, setting it back one block from the structure. In this example the combination is set so levers one, three and five open the door, but you can choose whatever combination you like, simply by linking the relevant redstone.

6

Stack two blocks in front of the repeaters and add a redstone torch at the front of the highest block.

7

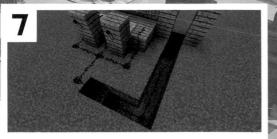

Dig a two-block-deep trench up to the door frame, leaving one block at the start. Place redstone, but stop two blocks from the end of the trench.

8

Add one block at the end of the redstone line. Place a redstone torch on the side of the block that faces the door frame.

9

Hide the redstone line, but leave the first two block lengths of the trench open. Place the metal door in its frame.

10

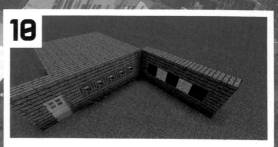

Finally, if you plan to use this in an adventure map, don't forget to place a clue somewhere so the player can work out the combination!

ONSEN RYOKAN

THE GAME

Onsen Ryokan was created for a newly established server, and was designed to provide entertainment for the guests while the server owner waited for others to join. Several interesting spots with 'Easter eggs' are placed around the spawn so guests will naturally explore the area without being coaxed.

Yuki Lin (aka 'Pigonge') describes the original server as a rather badly made and very small portal hub with flat walls and minimal decoration. He began expanding the build, based on a Japanese theme. However, this was Yuki's first attempt at a Japanese-themed building and the ceiling proved very difficult – he made several mistakes with the block count and ultimately had to take down a large section of the building and remake it.

At the moment, Yuki's unhappy with the number of Easter eggs in the game and plans to add more attractive locations to the spawn so he can place more eggs. He also plans to revisit the Japanese theme for his next build – a hot spring town.

THE BUILDER

A friend introduced Architecture student Yuki to Minecraft® some years ago. Since then he has dedicated a lot of his spare time to designing modern buildings within the game and is inspired by real-world creations that he can take and reimagine in Minecraft.

Although he is a dedicated community member and loves to share his builds with others, Yuki has no ambitions to be a game designer; for him, it's all about the design and building potential that the game provides and its use as an architectural tool.

Type of game: Server spawn/Easter
egg hunt
Difficulty: Easy
Time to play: 1–2 hours

Shaders and mods used: Sonic Ether's
Unbelievable Shaders, Sildur's Vibrant
Shaders, Conquest 1.8 Texture Pack
Time to build: 1 week (plus additional
buildings by yamatomotomoto and chibiaki0909)

CONSTRUCTION TIPS

Building in Minecraft® isn't like building in the 'real' world, so don't tie yourself to conventional ideas:

Create landscapes that aren't commonly seen in real life. In *Onsen Ryokan*, hot springs have been placed at different heights to create a fantastical Japanese-style world.

Make multiple identical spaces for hiding things in; it is quick to do and a great way to hide surprises!

Place buildings in spots slightly away from the main activity area. This encourages players to travel in broad sweeps and therefore gives you more flexibility in your Easter egg arrangements.

Open areas inside buildings always make interesting accents to closed spaces. Decorate these areas well to indicate that players can walk inside them.

THE JUGGLERS BALLS

THE GAME

The Jugglers Balls is a light-hearted adventure that tells the story of a juggler who has lost his balls – it's up to you, the player, to help him on his quest to find them. As the title suggests, there are plenty of rather silly jokes within the map and the builder's intention was to see how many embarrassing and naughty things he could get YouTubers to say while playing through the map.

The Jugglers Balls is a simple map, which can – and should – be completed without any deaths. The instructions are clear and easy to understand, and it's almost impossible to fail the map, although you can die (the builder, Jigarbov, has seen that happen a handful of times). More typically, though, a player gets through the entire story without much resistance. This is because the aim was more about telling a good story without sacrificing or distracting the player, and keeping the playtime under 20 minutes.

The idea for the game came after Jigarbov had been messing around with some of Minecraft®'s then-new commands. The builder thought he might be able to manipulate blocks using this new tech to make it look as if someone is juggling, and with a lot of work he managed to make it happen.

After showing off an early version online, lots of players made suggestions for improvements, including adding more balls and including different juggling styles. A few versions (and a lot of silly jokes) later, Jigarbov decided to make a full map, assisted by 'Abootflock'.

Although he likes the map, it wasn't as popular with the community as Jigarbov had hoped; while those who played it had a good time, it turned out that the game really was too easy. More importantly, the methods used to make the magic happen meant it didn't run smoothly on a lot of computers. Making sure a map will function on lower-end computers, as well as being optimised and fancy enough to get the most out of a good computer, is something that Jigarbov and many other popular mapmakers battle with constantly – with *The Jugglers Balls* that proved to be a problem, and is something he's been wary of ever since.

Type of game: Adventure
Difficulty: Easy
Time to play: 20 minutes

Number of players: 1-4
Shaders and mods used: MCEdit
Time to build: 20 hours

PUZZLE
SOLVING

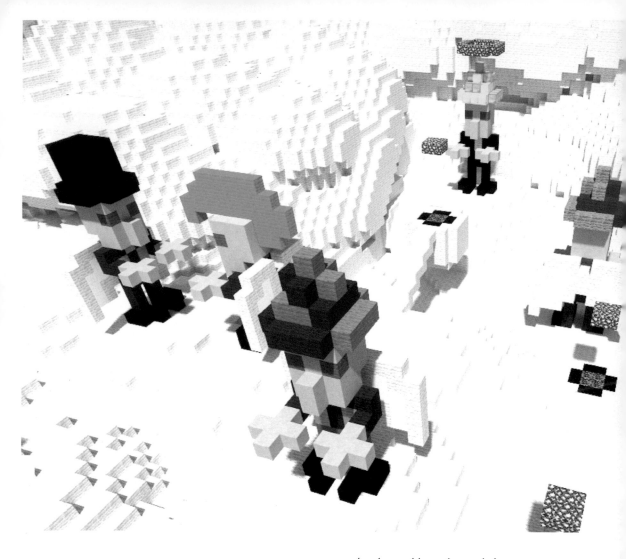

THE BUILDER

Jigarbov is a longstanding Minecraft® adventure builder, who has found great success with his *City of Love* map, among others. The Minecraft 1.7 update marked a new era for Jigarbov's style of mapmaking, with the functionality of command blocks allowing players to create and destroy blocks at will anywhere in the world.

The Jugglers Balls was the first time that Jigarbov actively outsourced the creation of his buildings and had someone custom build what was needed to make the map look great. He knew exactly the kind of map he wanted – a small-scale build showing off some cool tech – and knew he needed to create a great player experience. For this he enlisted the help of 'Abootflock' and outlined his vision of an enclosed space with three major points of interest: a farm, a futuristic building and a circus tent.

Abootflock built the areas to Jigarbov's spec, sending draft versions for approval before making the final builds. Throughout the process, Jigarbov felt it was important to have a clear vision and describe exactly what he wanted, worried that if he didn't give enough information then he might end up with something he didn't want or need, and waste a lot of time in the process.

JUGGLER

Special effects are important in modern Minecraft® maps. As maps get more complicated, and people consistently increase the quality of their in-game experiences, the competition becomes harder, so you have to do more to keep yourself on top. If you've got some special effects there's a good chance people will share your build with someone else, so in this tutorial we'll build a juggler step-by-step – then you can watch him juggle all day!

1

Start by building the legs, using whichever colours you like.

2

Next, add the juggler's torso and arms. We're using white-stained hardened clay for the skin colour here.

3

Now the face. Use special colours for the eyes – you could use red if you want an evil juggler! Put on his hat, and don't forget to give him some balls to juggle with. Use iron blocks for these, and put them in both hands.

4

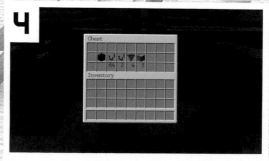

You will now need some repeaters, hoppers, comparators, redstone blocks and command blocks. You can get them all from the creative menu, but for command blocks you have to use: /give @p command_block.

5

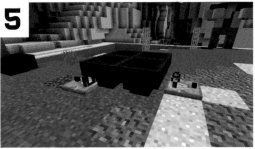

Lay down four hoppers so they are feeding into each other like a circle. You will need to hold shift when placing each one against the other. Now, if you put an item in one of the hoppers you should see it moving around to each hopper at a time. Place down comparators as shown. If you did the hoppers right you should see them flicking on and off, one after the other.

6

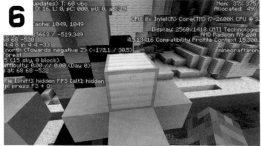

Next, press 1-3 and get the coordinates of the two iron balls the juggler will be juggling. Hover the crosshairs over them and note the 'x y z' coordinates given on the 'Looking at:' line.

7

Enter the following codes into each command block, substituting 'x y z' for the coordinates of your own balls:
/summon FallingSand x y z {Block:iron_block,DropItem:0,Motion:[-0.2,0.62,0.0]} / summon FallingSand x y z {Block:iron_block,DropItem:0,Motion:[0.2,0.62,0.0]}.

8

The juggler's balls may have moved, but take them from him for now so he has nothing in his hands.

JUGGLER

9

Depending on the orientation of the juggler, the Motion tag might need to be adjusted. Its format is 'Motion:[x,y,z]' and the numbers used are for the velocity and direction of the ball being thrown. You should be able to see a ghost ball in each hand and the direction it will fly – adjust if needed.

10

Now you're going to give the balls back to the juggler. Place repeaters as shown, and right-click them so their delay is set at the longest possible. In each command block write /setblock x y z iron_block, where 'x y z' are the coordinates of one of the balls you got previously. They should all be the same.

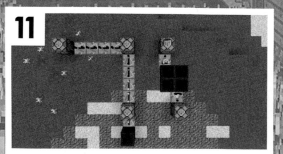

11

Now you have everything laid out, the ghost blocks in the juggler's hands should look correct and the comparators at the hoppers should be blinking. Place a redstone block at the start of your repeaters and...

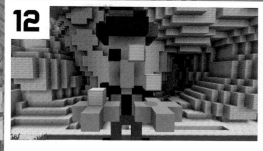

12

...now he is juggling! He'll do this forever, until you stop the command blocks. Have fun juggling!

JIGARBOV'S TIPS

TIP 1

Don't take things too seriously! People typically play
Minecraft® for fun, and if your storytelling is too
dark and depressing it might turn people off from
having a good time (or even playing your game to
start with).

TIP 2

While it's important not to compromise on your vision
for your map, bear in mind that people will play it, so
it needs to be functional, as well as look good.

TIP 3

If you're looking to build your mapmaking reputation
in the Minecraft community, include your online
name in the map itself. This will help people search
out your other work.

SURGEON SIM

THE GAME

Surgeon Sim was inspired by the PC game, *Surgeon Simulator*, which was originally created in 48 hours at a game jam event. In Minecraft®, John Blackhills's version plays out as a minigame, where you save sick patients across a variety of levels with different puzzles, secrets and stories. Beating a level gains you experience points, which you can spend on better operating tools in the surgeon shop. You need these to defeat enemies, clear blocks and solve the puzzles you will face in later levels.

Surgeon Sim isn't meant to be a very difficult game. It can take half an hour the first time it's played, but once you understand the logic and the tricks you'll be able to make your way through it much more smoothly – level 10 is the biggest challenge, so watch out for that one!

While he's made many games, *Surgeon Sim* is the one that John is most proud of and the one he considers his main project. At the moment it always takes top priority, but he looks forward to coming up with an even better idea and making a game that will outshine it.

THE BUILDER

John loves to create, whether it's putting together website videos, constructing 3D models, graphic design, or, of course, developing Minecraft games. When his cousin introduced him to Minecraft via YouTube videos, John wasn't very impressed or interested, but this changed when he downloaded the game for himself to take a closer look at what all the fuss was about.

Games hold a great deal of importance for John and he dreams of being a game designer professionally one day. While he's known for his adventure maps, he likes to build other things in Minecraft as well, such as houses and cities. What really makes John happy, though, is seeing other people playing with his creations; creating Minecraft maps can be very hard work, but the payoff comes from making other people happy.

Type of game: Minigame
Difficulty: Medium
Time to play: 20–30 minutes
Number of players: 1 or more

Shaders and mods used: Sildur's Basic
Shaders v1.05
Time to build: 90 hours (so far)

PUZZLE
SOLVING

JOHN'S TIPS

TIP 1

Every good adventure map should have some command blocks with commands such as /say, /tp, and /give. Take some time to learn how to use them, as they can add a lot to any adventure.

TIP 2

Redstone wires can be tricky to use if you only have a small space. Use half blocks or stairs with redstone placed on them to save room.

TIP 3

When you are using command blocks with the command /say (your text) you will see an @ symbol in chat. You can change this symbol to whatever text you want by putting your command block into an anvil and changing its name from 'Command Block' – you will see this text in chat instead of the @ symbol.

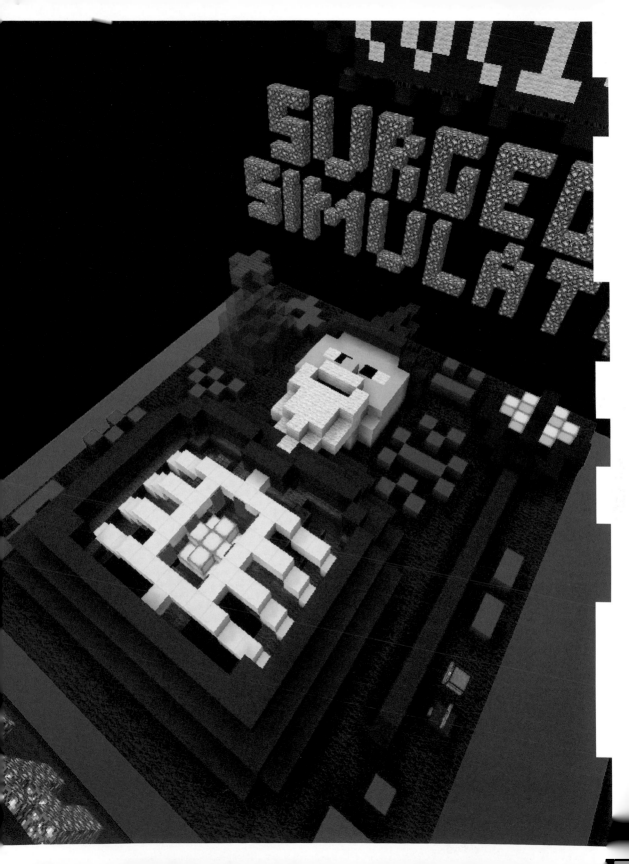

KINGDOM OF LORLAKE

THE GAME

Kingdom of Lorlake is set in medieval times and is filled with quests, stories and battles. The builder, MrBatou, doesn't know exactly how many quests there are in the map, but it definitely takes a long time to see all of the content. The main crux of the questing is exploration and his advice is to search everywhere and everything in the map!

Originally, MrBatou planned to make a city on water, but partway through he changed focus and decided to build an enormous castle instead. Overall, he's pleased with the result and has learned many lessons that he can take on to other builds, although he's certain that his next project will be more futuristic!

THE BUILDER

MrBatou is a Computing student from Dijon, France, who loves drawing and making music – you could simplify his greatest pleasure down to the idea that he loves creating something out of nothing.

MrBatou says he started playing Minecraft® 'just like everyone; in Survival mode.' As time went by he watched others create incredible things from little cubes and modestly says he just imitated them. He eventually joined a number of teams, including Elysium Fire, a large French team specialising in time-lapse building, and Deep Academy, which is dedicated to creating ultrarealistic builds.

MrBatou has a soft spot for futuristic and industrial builds, but his ideas and mood changes rapidly – he can easily turn his hand to anything from modern buildings to medieval architecture!

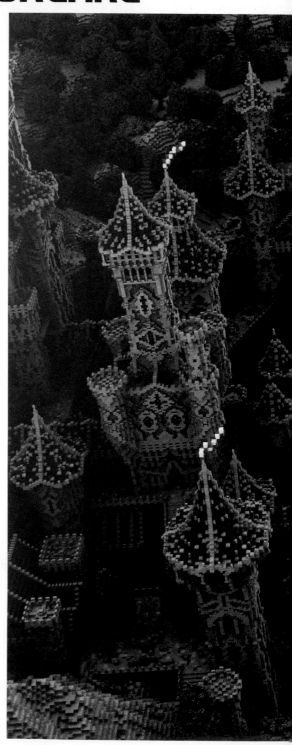

Type of game: MMORPG
Difficulty: Easy
Time to play: Months

Number of players: Unlimited
Shaders and mods used: KUDA Shaders
Time to build: 120 hours

PUZZLE SOLVING

MEDIEVAL TOWER AND WALL

There are a few basic structures that occur in most medieval builds, and if you can master the style of these then you are well on your way to making your own 'olde worlde' map! Here we're going to create a tower and wall.

1

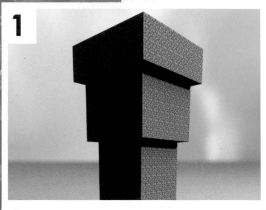

To make a medieval tower, start with a flared shape, as shown here.

2

Next, add pillars at the corners.

3

To finish your tower add details between the pillars, such as small buttresses, windows and battlements. Add a flag on top.

4

To make walls, start with a slightly flared shape, as shown. The bigger the wall is going to be, the more flared it should be.

5

As you did with the tower, add pillars to define the pattern.

6

Add smaller details, using the same elements as the tower so the styles work together. The materials you use are up to you – there's no perfect recipe.

With towers and walls you have the basics you need to create a medieval city: you just need to add some suitably styled buildings!

PUZZLE SOLVING: KINGDOM OF LORLAKE

Adding detail to your towers and walls adds texture and depth, which will increase the visual appeal of your builds.

THEFIX

THE GAME

TheFix is the first of three puzzle games in *TheFix* series, based on a clean and smooth block style. In part it was intended to allow players to experience the new features of Minecraft® 1.8, so it implements all of the 1.8 blocks across 16 different puzzles.

The game was released in 2014, and after just one week it had been downloaded over 500 times. What is perhaps even more remarkable is that the builder, 'Fr0zen Cookie', had no knowledge of command blocks or redstone before commencing his build. Creating the game therefore involved a lot of YouTube tutorials, watching how other puzzle maps functioned, and inviting friends to his server to test the different puzzles he had built himself.

In the beginning, the game was built in single-player mode because Fr0zen Cookie didn't want to waste money on a server. However, he quickly recognised that the map would make a better multiplayer game. Things didn't go exactly to plan, though, as a lot of his mechanics only worked with one player. As a result, it was impossible to play the complete map in the multiplayer game until he had changed a lot of his command block constructions.

Despite this, Fr0zen Cookie is really happy with his first map. Those areas that he would change have already been done and can be seen in his second puzzle map: *TheFix II*.

		PUZZLE
		SOLVING

Type of game: Puzzle
Difficulty: Medium
Time to play: About 2 hours
Number of players: Up to 4

Shaders and mods used.
Sildur's Vibrant Shaders, Replay Mod
Time to build: Too long!

THE BUILDER

Fr0zen Cookie is a gamer from Germany. While he was studying at college, he had a lot of time to watch YouTube videos and play games. He started out watching mapmaking videos by 'JesperTheEnd' and SethBling, reading Minecraft® resources and watching videos on command blocks, redstone and the Java programming language.

Like many builders, Fr0zen Cookie puts much of his Minecraft building skill down to playing with LEGO® as a child. He is passionate about introducing new ideas into the game. For him, games are the future of television, movies and books, although it's not something he wants to pursue as a career – as much as he loves playing around with blocks, Java and minigames, he doesn't want to sit in front of a computer all day. For Fr0zen Cookie, games are a hobby, not work.

FR8ZEN COOKIE'S TIPS

TIP 1
Three different command blocks are more than enough to handle the different actions and ideas of most mapmakers.

TIP 2
Although resource packs can transform Minecraft into a different game, sometimes it's nice to create a vanilla map.

TIP 3
Never give up. Sometimes it's hard to find a solution to a particular build problem, but Minecraft often has multiple ways of making things happen.

PASTEL DREAM

THE GAME

The adventure in *Pastel Dream* was an aside to the map's scenery, which was Yuki Lin's main focus. It was made so that the server's guests would be looking for 'Easter eggs' while walking around and familiarising themselves with the spawn.

Yuki takes the view that Easter egg hunting shouldn't be something that ever stresses the players; it should never be too hard to find the Easter egg, simply a nice way to discover new things as you explore the spawn. In a way, that means everything you see is an Easter egg – it's all new, and it's all a discovery!

Getting the colours right to make the glass look nice was particularly frustrating for Yuki, as was the challenge of getting the lighting right, because bare light sources immediately behind glass can be visually disturbing. Despite these challenges – or perhaps because of them – Yuki is really satisfied with how his Easter egg hunt motivates guests to walk around the spawn, and he wouldn't change anything in it.

THE BUILDER

Yuki is a Japanese Minecraft® builder whose interests revolve around music and architecture; his hobbies are playing violin and designing buildings, and he is currently studying Architecture at college (and plans to study music as well). His ambition comes from the desire to create things that will be remembered in the future and the notion that he can leave something of our time to be seen and understood in hundreds or even thousands of years.

Although Yuki enjoys being part of the Minecraft community and sharing his work with others, he mostly works alone when building.

Type of game: Easter egg hunt	Ether's Unbelievable Shaders,	PUZZLE
Difficulty: Easy	Sildur's Vibrant Shaders,	SOLVING
Time to play: Minutes	Conquest 1.8 Texture Pack	
Shaders and mods used: Sonic	Time to build: 3 days	

BUILDING TIPS

Pastel Dream offers a unique experience thanks to Yuki's unconventional use of building materials. Here is a selection of his build tips:

TIP 1

Don't be afraid to make wild decisions when it comes to block choices and themes. If you move away from classic themes and common block arrangements your builds will automatically become more unique.

TIP 2

Manage the height level of areas that are accessible to players. A playing area with height will always look more adventurous than a flat floor. Vegetation is also very important.

TIP 3

Geometric arrangements make good mazes, as players can easily lose their sense of where they are.

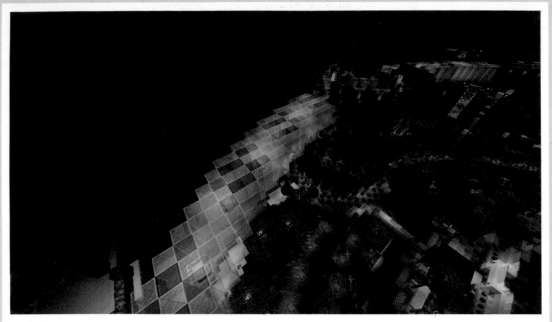

TIP 4

Create interesting pathways that will attract players. Due to their natural curiosity, this can be used to control where players are likely to go.

TIP 5

Allow players to look around the whole adventure area from a high viewing spot. This can function as a hint for your adventure.

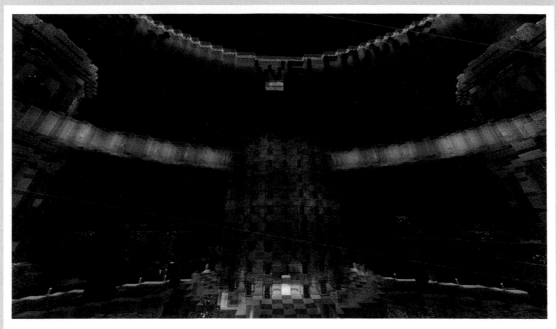

TIP 6
You don't know which texture pack your players will be using, so build things that look good when the default textures pack is used. That way, all your guests can explore an attractive world.

The most interesting learning point in *Pastel Dream* turned out to be how layered stained glass can be used to make a building that looks like it doesn't fully exist! Yuki plans to make some small-scale houses using the same technique.

JUST ESCAPE

THE GAME

The name of this puzzle game tells you almost everything you need to know about it: the simple premise is to 'escape' the map. Daniel's aim was to create a series of abstract levels that had a distinct Minecraft® shape, but were also pleasing to look at. Unlike many maps there is no storyline, no buildings, no rooms and no fighting. Instead, the player enters a world of platforms, jumps, postapocalyptic plants, flying objects and pipes, from which they must escape by solving puzzles.

The puzzles in the game aren't intellectually challenging, but you do have to be perceptive, patient and able to connect the threads. Your goal isn't only to play, but also to explore, which can extend the whole process. Daniel would certainly prefer it if you took the time to view his world, as he is particularly proud of its simply abstract quality, especially the fact that everything is created from the same elements, yet each level looks unique.

The reason behind the game is almost as intriguing as its design. Daniel didn't want to play Minecraft anymore, but one day he was struck by an idea that he wanted to share via his map with other players. The message that changed his life is hidden at the end of the map – it's your task to find it.

The build process wasn't long, although Daniel's initial design was – in his own words – 'awful'. However, once he had finalised the main theme everything became easier, and he's really pleased with the result. As the map is almost the same as the one he had in his mind he sees it as a success and wouldn't change a thing. In fact, he's so pleased with it that he is now building a continuation of the game in the form of single levels that he calls *Just Escape, In Pieces*.

Type of game: Puzzle/Escape
Difficulty: Medium
Time to play: 30-90 minutes
Number of players: You + friends!

Shaders and mods used: Sonic Ether's
Unbelievable Shaders
Time to build: 25 hours

PUZZLE
SOLVING

THE BUILDER

Daniel came across Minecraft® a few years ago during his school vacation. He immediately fell in love with its infinite creative options and unique atmosphere, and he always tries to emphasise its simple shapes in his maps. However, he isn't limited in what he will create, and doesn't concentrate on one style – for Daniel, diversity is good, and Minecraft is the ideal tool to bring the projects he imagines to life.

As an active member of the Minecraft community, Daniel feels it's good to share your work with others and to be inspired by other people's builds as well. However, he's a lone builder and doesn't work with a team; although he has worked with friends for a few days he's never been a member of a bigger team, and it's not something he has a desire to pursue.

COMMAND BLOCK SCREEN

The rules for building a screen like the ones appearing in *Just Escape* are the same, no matter how large or complicated the screen is. Here we will build a simple number screen using command blocks: if you understand how this works you will be able to create screens of your own.

1

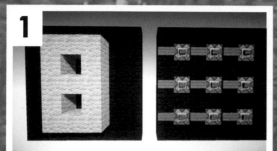

Build a board on which numbers from 1 to 9 will be displayed, as shown at the left. You will also need to make a keypad, remembering that it's important to place the buttons on command blocks (as shown at the right).

2

Take the coordinates of one of the three-block lines that will create the displayed number. We've picked the top line, which is shown in red wool here. Note that there are seven lines in total (three horizontal and four vertical).

3

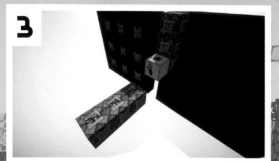

To build the first module set /setblock x y z wool in three vertical command blocks and /setblock x y z air in three horizontal blocks. In both cases, 'x y z' are the coordinates of each block in the line you picked in the previous step.

4

Set a redstone block as shown. The screen will show the line of coordinates you took (the top horizontal row in this example). When you destroy the redstone block the line will disappear.

5

Take the coordinates of the remaining six three-block lines (note that each of the lines overlaps at the ends).

6

Build six modules as outlined in step 3. You need one module for each line in the number display, and each module will need its own line coordinates.

7

Place redstone blocks as shown. Look closely at how this mechanism works: each module is responsible for one line in the display.

8

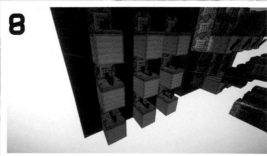

For the keypad, set iron blocks with repeaters on them. Repeaters are three times clicked and transmit signal FROM command blocks.

9

To build the module for the keypad set /setblock x y z air into the seven command blocks at the back of the display board, where 'x y z' are the coordinates of each redstone block from step 7. Set the same command into the final command block, but with coordinates of this module's redstone block. Then destroy it!

10

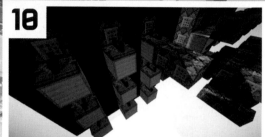

Set /setblock x y z redstone block into every command block on the keypad, where 'x y z' are the coordinates of the redstone block you added in step 9. Place two command blocks and redstone wire as shown.

11

Into the two command blocks you placed in step 10, set /setblock x y z redstone block, where 'x y z' are the coordinates of the redstone blocks in step 7 that power two vertical lines at the right (the lines that give the number 1 on the display).

12

Repeat the process of adding command blocks with redstone wire (and repeat step 11) for every number from 1 to 9 on the keypad. The number of command blocks (and the coordinates you use) will depend on which lines you need to trigger on the display.

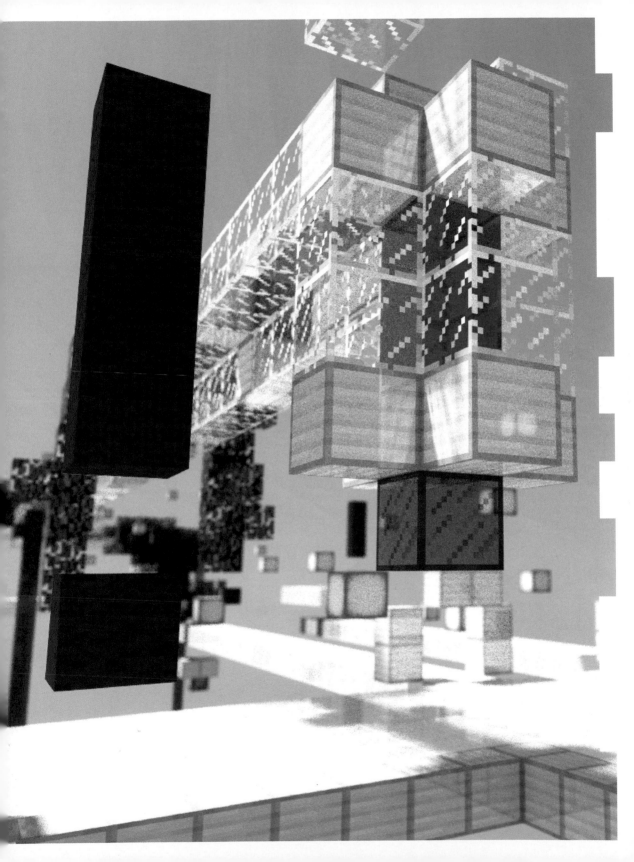

CONTRIBUTOR DIRECTORY

Cops vs. Robbers
Builder: Brauhaus der Hoffnung
Play: www.worldofminecraft.de
YouTube: www.youtube.com/user/
BrauhausTV

The Doctor
Builder: Sunfury
Play: www.planetminecraft.com/
member/sunfury
YouTube: www.youtube.com/user/
SunfuryCreative

The Beehive
Builder: goCreative
Play: www.go-creative.co

Tematos
Builder: Achi
Play: achi.ml

Sunaris
Builder: Sunfury
Play: www.planetminecraft.com/
member/sunfury
YouTube: www.youtube.com/user/
SunfuryCreative

Eronev Mansion Adventure
Builder: Tim Gehrig
Play: www.jigarbov.net
YouTube: www.youtube.com/user/jigarbov

The Asylum
Builder: Sunfury
Play: www.planetminecraft.com/
member/sunfury
YouTube: www.youtube.com/user/
SunfuryCreative

City of Love/City of Love 2
Builder: Tim Gehrig
Play: www.jigarbov.net
YouTube: www.youtube.com/user/jigarbov

Symbiosis
Builder: Everbloom Studios
Play: everbloomstudios.com

Junkyard Warfare
Builder: goCreative
Play: www.go-creative.co

Spaghetti Rollercoaster
Builder: Daniel Pe
Play: www.planetminecraft.com/
member/deliciouspancake

Emerald Heart
Builder: Baptiste Mauger
Play: //www.planetminecraft.com/
member/mrbatou/

Echoes from the Deep
Builder: Everbloom Studios
Play: everbloomstudios.com

Rollerquester
Builder: Hans Verdolaga
Play: www.planetminecraft.com/member/
destiny_gene

La Brocanterie
Builder: Schnogot
Play: www.planetminecraft.com/
project/la-brocanterie-48-players-
sg-map-feat-eti28/
YouTube: www.youtube.com/user/schnogot

Eronev 2: Soul Cauldron
Builder: Tim Gehrig
Play: www.jigarbov.net
YouTube: www.youtube.com/user/jigarbov

The Risen Dead
Builder: Sunfury
Play: www.planetminecraft.com/
member/sunfury
YouTube: www.youtube.com/user/
SunfuryCreative

Infinity Dungeon
Builder: Tim Gehrig
Play: www.jigarbov.net
YouTube: www.youtube.com/user/jigarbov

Cube Block
Builder: Simon Biebl
Play: www.planetminecraft.com/
project/cube-block-x3
YouTube: www.youtube.com/user/
XxRexRaptorxX

The Port of Frontier
Builder: Linscraft
Play: Server IP: LinsCraft.World
Web: www.linscraft.design

Crypte of the Death
Builder: Baptiste Mauger
Play: //www.planetminecraft.com/
member/mrbatou/

Navorath Valley
Builder: goCreative
Play: www.go-creative.co

Phain
Builder: Andrzej Czerniewski
Play: www.planetminecraft.com/project/
phain-game-board-of-the-ancients-6000-
x-6000-multiple-biomes-survival-map-923-
plots-theme---hexagons/

Foosball table
Builder: SethBling
Play: www.sethbling.com
YouTube: www.youtube.com/user/sethbling

MCBCon Arena
Builder: Everbloom Studios
Play: everbloomstudios.com
Twitter: @EverbloomEN

The Tourist
Builder: Loic Serra
Play: http://www.planetminecraft.com/
project/adventure-map-the-tourist/
YouTube: www.youtube.com/user/
OneManBand2a

Onsen Ryokan
Builder: Yuki Lin
Play: www.planetminecraft.com/
member/pigonge/
YouTube: www.youtube.com/user/
RYsDelight

The Jugglers Balls
Builder: Tim Gehrig
Play: www.jigarbov.net
YouTube: www.youtube.com/user/jigarbov

Surgeon Sim
Builder: John Blackhills
Play: calesk.7x.cz

Kingdom of Lorlake
Builder: Baptiste Mauger
Play: //www.planetminecraft.com/
member/mrbatou/

TheFix
Builder: Fr0zen Cookie
Play: www.planetminecraft.com/project/
thefix---minecraft-18-puzzle-map
YouTube: www.youtube.com/user/
Flash2Boom

Pastel Dream
Builder: Yuki Lin
Play: www.planetminecraft.com/
member/pigonge/
YouTube: www.youtube.com/user/
RYsDelight

Just Escape
Builder: Daniel Pe
Play: www.planetminecraft.com/
member/deliciouspancake

PICTURE CREDITS

INDEX

ABOUT THE AUTHOR

KIRSTEN KEARNEY has been a tech and computer games journalist for more than a decade. She began her career as a researcher and producer in broadcasting at the BBC. She has written reviews, columns and features for many of the digital entertainment magazines and websites in the UK and is the Editor-in-Chief of the highly successful games media website www.ready-up.net.

Kirsten has written a variety of in-depth pieces on various game genres and specific series and franchises over the last 10 years, but has a particular interest in Minecraft® and user-created content. She is also the author of the bestselling books *Create and Construct: Incredible Minecraft Cities* and *Create and Construct: Super Structures in Minecraft.*

ACKNOWLEDGEMENTS

For Louise Crawford. Thank you.

Special thanks to Michael Anderson, FreshMilkyMilk.

Writing about Minecraft has made me some very special young friends from all around the world. Your enthusiasm has been the best part of working on these books. Keep building, Nathan Bond Crawford McNiven, Liam Ruddy, Olivia Loughlin, Cian Thomson, Trinity Perdue, Matthias van der Linden, Sam Corbett and Mitchal Dowsett.